IMAGES of America

ARVIN, LAMONT, AND WEEDPATCH

The area draws in people looking for a better future. Dorothy and Lawrence Nourse were two of the early pioneers who moved to the area to farm. The rich soil made for productive farming, but they faced challenges including frost and lack of easy access to irrigation water. Their first attempt at farming in Arvin in the early 1900s failed, leaving them no choice but to relocate. They eventually returned, and their second attempt proved successful. They became integral members of the Arvin community.

On the Cover: Arvin residents gather for a photograph in the business district in the 1920s. This is only a third of the original panoramic photograph. It showcases the businesses (including A.J. Richardson's Shell service station), technology, and fashion of the era. (Courtesy of Don Burkett.)

IMAGES
of America

ARVIN, LAMONT, AND WEEDPATCH

Ruth Leon Barba with Mary Louise Durham
Foreword by Dr. James "Fizzer" Young

ARCADIA
PUBLISHING

ISBN 978-1-4671-0390-9

Published by Arcadia Publishing
Charleston, South Carolina

Printed in the United States of America

Library of Congress Control Number: 2019939907

For all general information, please contact Arcadia Publishing:
Telephone 843-853-2070
Fax 843-853-0044
E-mail sales@arcadiapublishing.com
For customer service and orders:
Toll-Free 1-888-313-2665

Visit us on the Internet at www.arcadiapublishing.com

Dedicated to my parents, Marta and Jesus Leon.
Gracias por su amor incondicional y todos los sacrificios
que han hecho para darnos un mejor futuro.

Contents

FOREWORD

This pictorial history tells the story of Arvin, Lamont, and Weedpatch, three small communities in the grand Central Valley of California. Over the past 100 years, these communities have experienced two great migrations of people from the southern plains and Mexico and Central America. The Great Depression, along with unusual climate changes including a severe drought and winds and dust, prompted a westward migration—particularly from Texas, Oklahoma, Arkansas, and Missouri—that for some ended in small towns and labor camps in the San Joaquin Valley. Di Giorgio Labor Camp 8 and Willet's Labor Camp housed newly arrived "Okies" and "Arkies," as the locals called them. Many of the migrants felt that the terms were degrading, but others wore them as a badge of recognition and togetherness with fellow migrants. Many found refuge at the Government Camp (Sunset Camp), which appeared in John Steinbeck's novel *The Grapes of Wrath*. The historic camp continues to serve migrant families working in agriculture. The 1960s marked the start of a second migration to the area. Individuals and families from Mexico and Central America replaced Dust Bowl migrants moving "back home" or to Bakersfield after their children finished high school in the 1950s and 1960s. Presently, the Latino population in each community surpasses 90 percent. Arvin was incorporated as a city in 1960. Lamont and Weedpatch remain under the jurisdiction or the Kern County Board of Supervisors. Since 1949, Arvin High School has been a common denominator among the three communities. All high school students in the area have attended Arvin High and participated in the same teams and school activities. Deep relationships have been cultivated over time and have kept the communities connected. May the vintage images of Arvin, Lamont, and Weedpatch in this book inspire the future generations of these thriving communities.

—James Clark Young, EdD
Chancellor Emeritus
Kern Community College District

ACKNOWLEDGMENTS

Writing this book has been a privilege, and sharing it with the wonderful people of Arvin, Lamont, and Weedpatch is a gift. Images and information were borrowed from various sources. Every effort was made to share the most trusted accounts. Any factual or interpretive errors were not intentional. This book was made possible because of the foresight of preservers of local history, including Eugene Burmeister, Don Burkett, Dorris Weddell, Mable Krauter, Dorothy Nourse, Mable Jobe, Joyce Robinson, John Martin, and others. I am grateful to Mary Louise Durham and Dr. James C. Young for the valuable help and guidance they provided me along the way. The following went above and beyond to help me gather images and information: the Board of Directors of the Arvin Historical Society, Sharon and Suzanne Garrison (Sunset Camp), Lori Wear (Kern County Museum), Kim O'Connor (Roman Catholic Diocese of Fresno), Amy Schmidt and staff of the Kern County Library, Rachel (Ozuna) Arias (the Sonoran Project), and Georgia Rhett (Arvin Union School District). Special thanks to my interviewees for sharing their stories and photographs: Don and Carol Burkett, Laverne Wernli, W.C. and Gwen Stampes, Labetta Glenn, Sylvia and Arnold Cattani, Mildred Blackburn, Charlene Tarver, Toni and Lupe Pichardo, Betty and J.R. Chagoya, Janie Jacques, Jesse Ortiz, Carmen Marquez, and Frank Wallace Reed. Stephen Pelz and Maria Guzman (Housing Authority), Millie Cadmus, County of Kern staff, Dr. Oliver Arthur Rosales, Tony Reed, the Lamont Assembly of God Church, and others generously provided assistance. Thank you to the wonderful staff at Arcadia Publishing. Special thanks to my PVRS team for their support and encouragement. I am grateful to my family for their help and support throughout this process. Most importantly, I thank my husband, Lloyd, for helping me tremendously and showering me with love, support, and encouragement every step of the way.

Mary would like to thank the Arvin Historical Society Board of Directors, including Laverne Wernli, Dean and Shirley Christian, Rick and Linda Leary, and Lupe and Toni Pichardo, for always being there to help find information for this book.

INTRODUCTION

The history of Arvin, Lamont, and Weedpatch is incredibly rich. This book tells the story of these communities using a thematic approach: early years, people and places, schools, faith, businesses and agriculture, and migrations and labor camps. It covers over 200 years of history from the 1770s to the 1970s. In every chapter, photographs and information about Arvin are presented first followed by Lamont and Weedpatch. These respective histories follow a chronological flow.

It is unknown who the first people of the land were, but it is believed the Yokut Indians inhabited the area for thousands of years. Over time, the native population declined as a result of various factors, including forced removal from their land. When the Spanish empire governed California from 1769 to 1821, padres were sent out to establish missions. Two of the first recorded European visitors to the area were Don Pedro Fages and Padre Francisco Garces. After gaining independence from Spain, Mexico governed California and issued land grants. Rancho el Tejon on the outskirts of Arvin was granted to Jose Antonio Aguirre and Ignacio del Valle in 1843. After the Mexican-American War (1846–1848), the Treaty of Guadalupe Hidalgo was signed, and the United States gained control of California.

Settlers from the United States and other parts of the world purchased land, established roots, and began farming. The soil was fertile; but without water, farming was limited. Settlers initially engaged in dry farming. The construction of the Eastside Canal in 1893 and the drilling of wells changed the game for early settlers. Water ensured the success of general and diversified farming. The land went from desert-like conditions to being, as Arvin's slogan reads, a "garden in the sun." The term "irrigated desert" perfectly captures what the area has become. Some successful small to average scale farms turned into agri-businesses and major employers in the area. Farmers consistently relied on a large and inexpensive labor force, which by the 1920s was primarily made up of ethnic Mexicans. The growth in population in the 1930s caused by the Dust Bowl migration brought changes to the area. Dust Bowl migrants, fleeing hunger and despair, traveled westward clinging to the promise of a new and prosperous life. The life of early migrant laborers was characterized by a constant search for jobs and life in labor camps. Over time, some migrants decided to permanently settle in the area, but others moved away. Mexican laborers fleeing economic woes and the aftermath of civil unrest sought employment opportunities in the United States. Some participated in guest worker programs like the Bracero Program while others came on their own terms. To feed the nation abundantly and themselves only meagerly, many had to endure unequal access to goods and services, unforgiving working conditions, and unfair wages. Despite the challenges, they continued to come, and some settled in the area indefinitely. Arvin, Lamont, and Weedpatch underwent another dramatic transformation in the 1980s and 1990s when the white population, which once constituted the majority, was replaced by thousands of Mexicans and Central Americans. Arvin's current population exceeds 20,000, and Lamont is not far behind. Over 90 percent of the population in all three communities is Latino.

This book attempts to share the stories of key individuals and groups who shaped the area's history. Although history is the full completed past, it has not been fully told and recorded. The history of the native people of this area is a case in point. More is known about the Spanish explorers than about the natives. Another example is the lack of historical writings about early Mexicans, African Americans, and other groups. Where written sources have been few, oral histories and photographs have been the primary means of telling the past. This book seeks to spark curiosity about the past and inspire community members to preserve and share their stories, pictures, and artifacts. As we look to the future, it is important to recognize that countless stories are waiting to be told. Who will preserve and author the history of the area in the years to come?

—Ruth Leon Barba

One

The Early Years

The Yokuts inhabited the area for thousands of years. They camped and hunted in the area presently known as Weedpatch, in which kangaroo rats, jackrabbits, and rattlesnakes roamed freely. The Kitanemuk (Tejon Indians) lived along the southern tip of the San Joaquin Valley in the Sierra Nevada Mountains. Throughout their history, they fought for the right to remain on their ancestral land. Early European settlers labeled them *tejon*, "badger" in Spanish. In 1853, the Sebastian Indian Reservation was established and overseen by Edward F. Beale. He bought Rancho el Tejon in 1863, and only 100 of 2,000 native people remained on the land. Many of the Tejon natives who stayed on the land were affected by the 1952 earthquake and had to relocate. Pictured is an Indian family in front of an adobe building and a wigwam on the reservation. (Courtesy of the Library of Congress.)

From 1769 to 1821, California was under Spanish colonial rule. Don Pedro Fages passed through Rancho el Tejon in 1772, and in 1776, Padre Francisco Garces was in the area on his way through the San Joaquin Valley. Pictured is California Registered Historical Landmark No. 371 (Francisco Garces O.F.M.), located in the courtyard of Saint Thomas the Apostle Church in Arvin. (Both, courtesy of Martha Leon.)

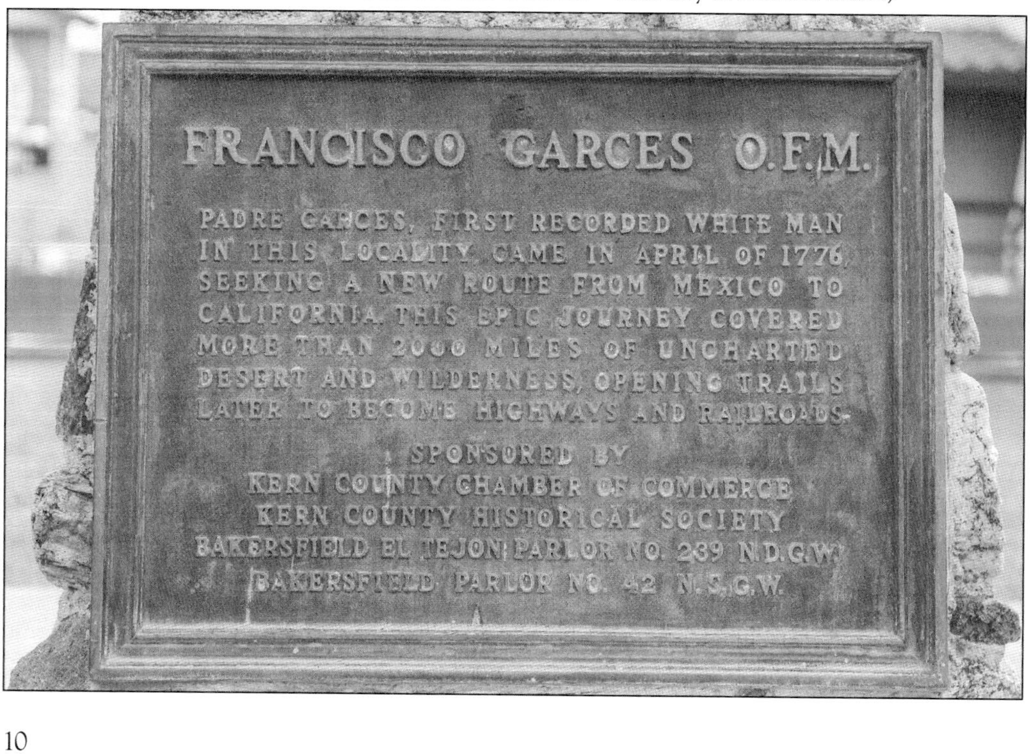

In 1821, Mexico achieved independence from Spain and governed California until 1846. During those years, Mexican *rancheros* managed land granted by governors of California. East of Arvin on White Wolf Grade stood a house that was once part of the 97,616-acre Rancho el Tejon. Gov. Manuel Micheltorena, the last Mexican governor sent to California from Mexico City, granted the land to Jose Antonio Aguirre and Ignacio del Valle on November 24, 1843. The Mexican-American war broke out in 1846, and in 1848, the Treaty of Guadalupe Hidalgo was signed and the area became part of the United States. Two years later, in 1850, California became the 31st state in the Union. (Above, courtesy of Martha Leon; below, courtesy of the Arvin Historical Society.)

According to historian William Harland Boyd, there were three stages of settlements in the area: homesteading with dry farming, general farming, and diversified farming. In 1891, farmers cultivated 40,000 acres of grain from Arvin to Weedpatch. Above, a Mr. Roderick and an unidentified girl stand next to a mound of hay in 1921. Pictured below is a team of horses used to haul hay. General farming was made possible in part by the Eastside Canal, constructed in 1893 by E.M. Roberts. (Both, courtesy of the Arvin Historical Society.)

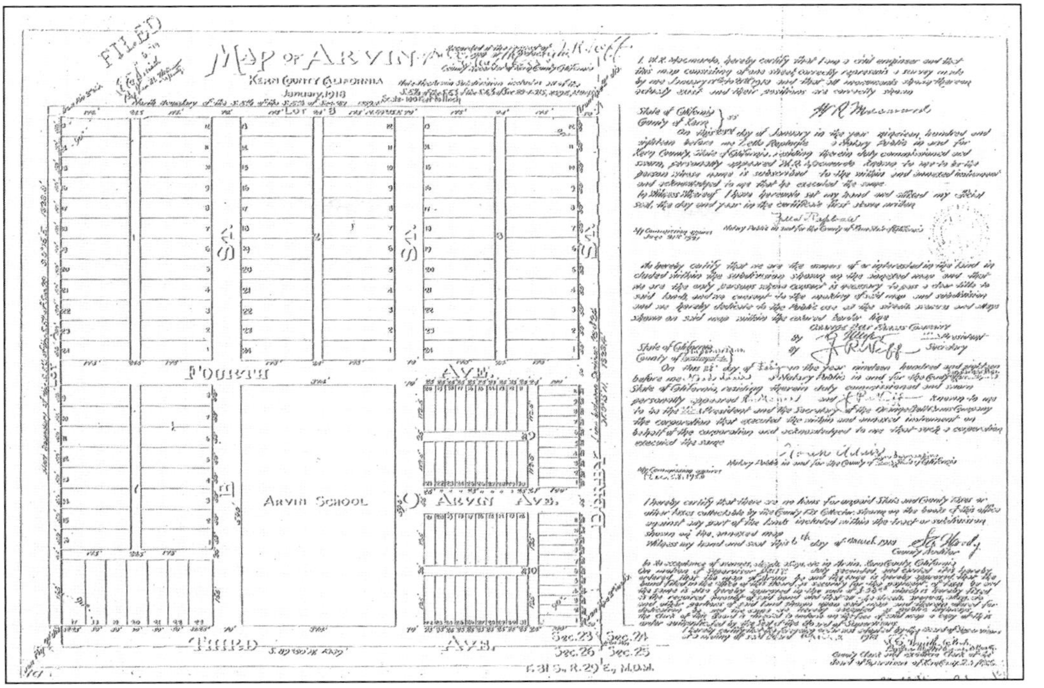

In November 1907, the Foothill Citrus Farms Corporation, comprised of people mostly from San Bernardino, sold 440 acres in the area and formed a "colony" in present-day Arvin. A.N. Habecker and Ralph Haven, along with their families, are believed to be the first settlers of this colony. One account states that J.D. Tucker arrived in Section 26 (Arvin townsite) in 1906. He was the engineer of Foothill Citrus Farms and opened Weedpatch Nursery in 1909, effectively pioneering the fruit tree industry. Initially, the Habeckers lived in a tent on what is now Di Giorgio Park. Haven built the first house and planted 10 acres of fruit trees. The colony grew to include the Richardson, Neff, and other families by 1911. The townsite was surveyed by 1914. B Street, C Street, Third Avenue, Fourth Avenue, Arvin Avenue, and Derby Street are visible on the 1918 tract map of the townsite above. Pictured below is the Maddux family's first home around 1915. (Above, courtesy of Kern County Public Works; below, courtesy of the Arvin Historical Society.)

The Eastside Canal furnished irrigation water to 16,000 acres in the area, but it was located about four miles away from Arvin. Deepwater wells were drilled in Arvin to meet the various needs for water. The first irrigation well was built by Arvin Richardson, George Richardson, J.D. Tucker, and Ralph Haven in 1910. Pictured here is a man drilling for water in the 1920s. (Courtesy of the Arvin Historical Society.)

By 1911, Arvin was plugged into the modern world of electricity. The colony grew quickly and had 28 houses by 1914. A total of 75 people populated the colony in 1915, including 41 adults, 9 teenagers, and 25 children. They built homes using one-by-twelve-inch boards and covered cracks with batts, which did little to protect against the frequent dust storms. Lawrence Packard captured the photograph of the townsite above from a tank in 1922. Pictured below is the Nourse family home in 1920. (Both, courtesy of the Arvin Historical Society.)

In 1916, the Arvin Farm Center took first place at the Kern County Fair. To celebrate the victory, a community barbecue was organized. The barbecue was well attended and included a band

(pictured at right). Third Avenue is visible in the background, with Bear Mountain School at center. (Courtesy of the Arvin Historical Society.)

Arvin is named after George Arvin Richardson. He was a farmer, businessman, and pioneer in the field of irrigation. His involvement in the civic life of the community and his many contributions won him the esteem of his fellow residents. He was known for helping people farm, selling land for a fair price, loaning machinery, and creating pipelines. When the town needed a name, Birdie Heard submitted several on behalf of the townspeople including Heard, Arvin, and Bear Mountain to the US postmaster general, and Arvin was selected. Arvin moved to Bakersfield in 1920. He was married to Hattie, and they had two daughters named Elizabeth and Jane. Arvin died on July 2, 1951, at the age of 68. He is buried at Greenlawn Memorial Park Northeast in Bakersfield. (Courtesy of the Arvin Historical Society.)

George Richardson, the father of Arvin, moved to the colony with his family around 1907 from San Bernardino. The family farmed and owned a service station. George was married to Millie, and they had six children. The Richardson family is seen here in 1938. From left to right are (first row) Forest Rushing, Fanny, George, Millie, and Clara; (second row) Carl, Myrtle, Myra, and Arvin. Fanny gave birth to William Arvin Tanner, the first baby born in the colony, on May 8, 1911. (Courtesy of the Arvin Historical Society.)

Prior to 1914, mail was delivered to Weedpatch Corner and residents who visited picked up the mail for the entire colony. The system was not efficient, and Warder Nance was hired to carry mail from Edison to the colony. In 1913, Birdie Heard arrived in Arvin and lobbied for a post office. The post office (pictured above) was established in July 1914 on what became Jake Krauter's property on the corner of Hood Street and Walnut Drive. Jake Krauter is pictured below using his combine harvester in 1921. Birdie Heard became the first postmistress. The post office was later moved to Staple's Arvin Store. In the late 1920s, Effie Mahin, "the Lady from Arvin," began working as a rural mail carrier. During the war years, she took great pride in delivering correspondence from service members to their families. A new post office was opened in Arvin in 1953. Arvin began using the 93203 zip code in 1963. In 1976, a memorial with the names of postmasters up to 1953 was erected at the site of the original post office. (Both, courtesy of the Arvin Historical Society.)

Early Arvin settler Otto Wernli immigrated from Switzerland and farmed the fertile land. He married Lena, and they built their first home together in 1915 on Haven Drive. Lena and her daughter Anna are pictured near a vineyard of Thompson seedless grapes. Lawrence, the son of Otto and Lena, married Laverne, and they built a house on Haven Drive next to his childhood home. Lawrence, a well-respected member of the community, passed away in 2009. (Courtesy of Laverne Wernli.)

By 1915, Arvin boasted a population of 75. Early residents are pictured in front of the Bear Mountain School, where church services were also held. Edgar Combs, an early resident, identified Ralph and Effa Haven (indicated with marks over their heads). It is likely that members of the Adams, Gregory, Habecker, Heard, Krauter, Richardson, Smith, Tucker, Warder, and Wernli families are in the photograph as well. Many streets in Arvin bear the names of these pioneers. (Courtesy of Don Burkett.)

In 1914, the first public library in Arvin was located on the corner of Hood Street and Walnut Drive. By 1917, the library was located at Staple's Arvin Store. On January 1, 1927, the Kern County Library opened its Arvin Branch. Mrs. Cook was the librarian, followed by a Mrs. Seat. A new building was constructed in 1938. The current building opened on October 17, 1997, at 201 Campus Drive. The library has been a gathering place for families and children since its inception. (Courtesy of Kern County Library.)

The Saylor and Maddux families were among the first to establish residency in the town. Pictured at left are Haley and Eliza Saylor in 1908. Haley is believed to have been the first blacksmith in town. The Arvin garage and blacksmith shop was established by Rivers and Renner by 1922. Below, the Maddux family is enjoying a picnic and wildflowers in the 1920s. (Both, courtesy of the Arvin Historical Society.)

From 1858 to 1861, the Kern River Slough Station was in operation on the Butterfield Overland Stage route. It was approximately three miles west of Lamont on Panama Road and south of this marker. The route ran from St. Louis, Missouri, to San Francisco until the outbreak of the Civil War. The marker was registered and dedicated in 1957. Eugene Burmeister wrote that travelers were served goat flesh and coffee at the Sinks of Tejon Station (Historical Landmark No. 540) on their way to the Kern River Slough Station. (Author's collection.)

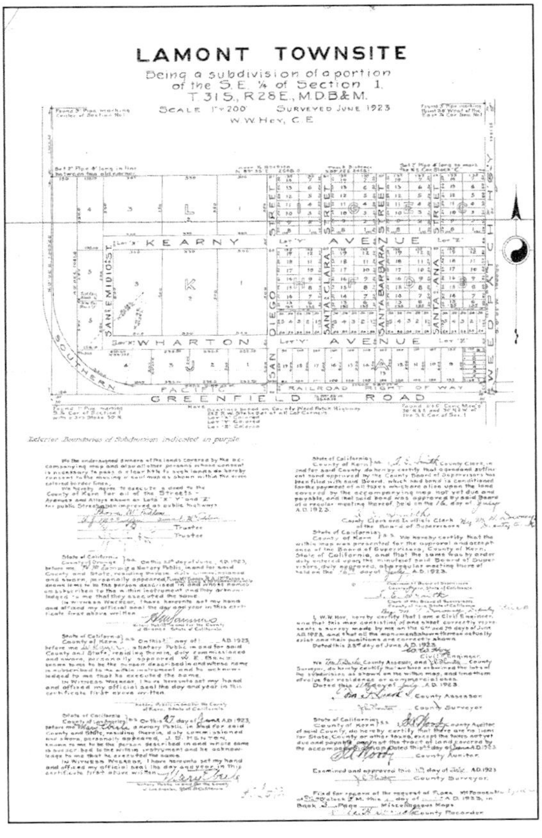

Settlers arrived in the Lamont area in the 1880s. It was officially surveyed in 1874. The town was founded in 1923 by Arthur McFadden, who subdivided 20 acres of land that year. There are two stories of how Lamont received its name. One is that Harry Thompson asked McFadden to give his property a Scottish name and McFadden choose Lamont after his family clan. The other story is that McFadden named the town after his daughter Anna Lamont McFadden. Some of the early settlers were from the Cattani, Clendenen, Thompson, Thornburgh, and Wilson families. S.E.L. Wharton was referred to as the "father of Lamont" and is credited with laying out the townsite. (Courtesy of Kern County Public Works.)

Yokut Indians camped and hunted in the Weedpatch area for thousands of years. In 1874, the site was surveyed and named Weed Patch because of the abundance of weeds. The name is presently spelled "Weedpatch." Early settlers made their profits in the cattle and dry farming industry. Hay baling is underway at the S.A. Hall Farm in Weedpatch in this 1915 photograph. (Courtesy of the Kern County Museum.)

Joseph Cuda and Calvin Alexander were two of the first settlers in Weedpatch. Alexander moved to Weedpatch in 1893 and bought 80 acres. Grapes and figs were among the first crops grown in the area. The corner of Weedpatch Highway and Buena Vista Boulevard became known as Alexander's corner (pictured around the 1920s). The Marion Franklin Parish General Merchandise store is at right. Weedpatch was a small community made up of only a few homes and businesses. In 1924, a road was built connecting it to Arvin. In 1925, the annual Weedpatch District Fair drew over 3,000 people. Farmers like Joseph Cuda, Joseph Di Giorgio, E.D. Mitchell, and A.F. Kirkland put their best products on display. Weedpatch also had its own church named the Thompson Memorial Church. In 1921, the church's Ladies' Aid group created the *Souvenir Cook Book*, which included a brief history of Weedpatch. (Courtesy of the Kern County Museum.)

Two

PEOPLE AND PLACES

Vehicles of the time are seen riding on Bear Mountain Road (California Highway 223) in this iconic photograph from 1920. The new highway provided easy access in and out of town. State Route 223 connects travelers headed westbound to State Route 99 and those headed eastbound to State Route 184. In 2012, the portion of the highway from State Route 99 to State Route 58 was designated part of the Purple Heart Trail, a network of roads across the United States that honors Purple Heart recipients. (Courtesy of the Kern County Museum.)

From left to right, a Mr. Clardy, Henry G. Clardy, and Mrs. Clardy pose between their cotton patch and home on Stockton Avenue in Arvin in 1921. The Clardy residence typifies the landscape aesthetics of the earliest Arvin homes. (Courtesy of Don Burkett.)

In Arvin and Lamont, paid airplane rides were available on Sundays. The airplanes in this photograph were on Derby Street in Arvin in the 1920s. (Courtesy of Don Burkett.)

John W. and George Holt stand beside their vine-covered cottage in Arvin in 1920. John served as the Kern County supervisor for the 2nd District from 1951 to 1971. He was preceded by Perry Brite (1929–1934) and followed by George Parish (1935–1938), C.W. Harty (1939–1950), and David Head (1971–1982). (Courtesy of Don Burkett.)

In small, modest steps, Arvin moved toward modernization. Edgar Combs introduced the first washing machine to Arvin. Wilburn and Birdie Heard are pictured here with the machine. (Courtesy of the Arvin Historical Society.)

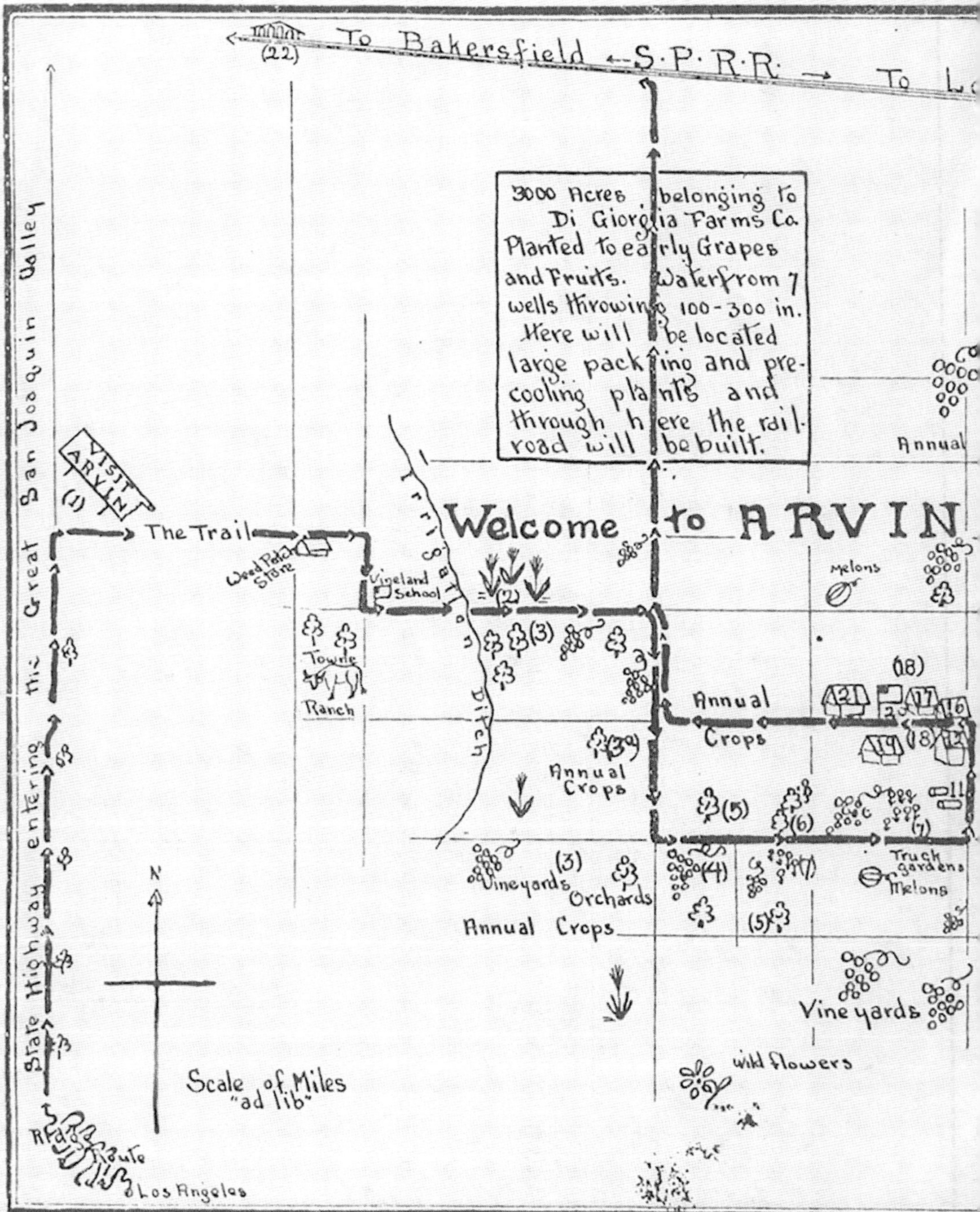

This map by Arvin resident Dorothy Nourse was printed in the May 29, 1922, *Arvin Booster* newspaper. Nourse was an active member of the community and preserved local history through photography, drawings, and written accounts. She donated her collection to the

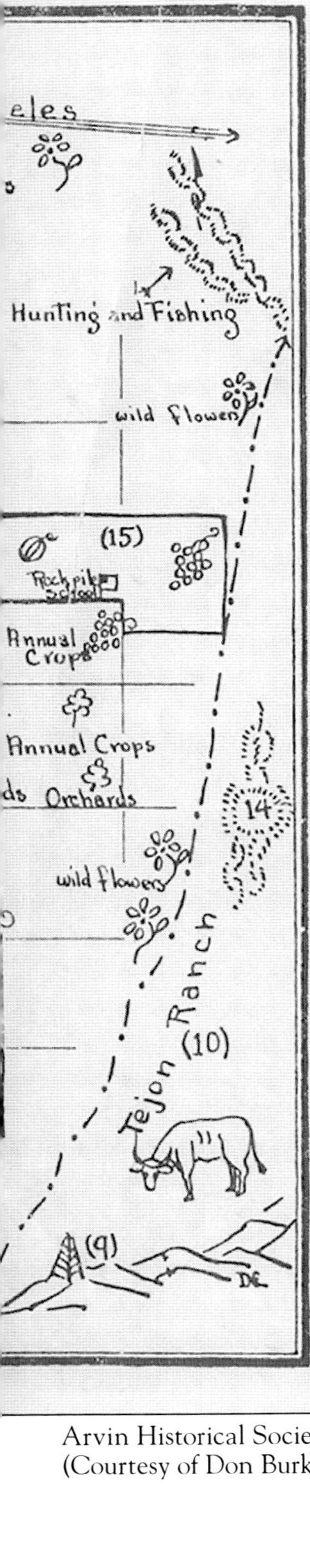

Arvin Historical Society

POST OFFICE BOX 96
ARVIN, CALIFORNIA 93203

KEY TO MAP

1. Sign erected by the ARVIN BOOSTERS' CLUB marks the point where Caravan leaves the State Highway in order to see the Earlist Fruit Lands of the San Joaquin Valley.

2. This section has been for years one of the favorite grazing and dry farming districts. But—

3. Within the last four years the value of the land for early fruits is fast changing the grain lands into vineyards and orchards.

3a. Farm section of land recently acquired by H. F. Wilson, president of the California Peach Growers' Association.

4. This is one of ARVIN'S small vineyards, yielding in its fourth year 6½ tons of early fruit to the acre.

5. This section is known as "The Colony." Here small landholders have united in order to develop water for all at the lowest figure.

6. One of the oldest orchards in Arvin. Twelve-year-old trees yielding a big tonnage of early, juicy apples.

7. Nurseries propagating grapes and budded trees for next season's planting.

8. Three hundred and twenty acres planted to early Malaga grapes by the Di Giorgio Farms Company.

9. Comanche Point, 7 miles south of the Arvin townsite, marks the point of union between the Coast Range and the Sierra Nevada Mountains. On this point the Comanche Oil Company is putting down its first well on its 4100-acre lease from the Tejon Ranch Company.

10. The 283,000-acre Tejon cattle ranch. In one of its canyons is the Tejon Indian Reservation.

11. Pipe yards for the making of irrigating pipe, which plays an important part in the new developments.

12. ARVIN Service Station and Realty Office.

13. This is another "colony" of small landholders united to develop water.

14. Bear Mountain, Sentinel of Arvin, over a mile in height.

15. The 1900-acre ranch owned by Wylie B. Giffen, president of the Sun-Maid Raisin Association, which is being planted to grapes and which, with smaller acreages, will help to produce Arvin's large tonnage of early melons and sweet potatoes.

16. Garage and Blacksmithy.

17. The Arvin Store and Post Office.

18. Arvin Townsite. Here the Caravaners will receive some of Arvin's fruits to cheer them along the trail.

19. Hotel and Restaurant.

20. The Arvin School, also used for church services and social gatherings.

21. The Arvin Long Staple Cotton Gin, which ginned local cotton sent to Europe under the Toll Plan and reported to have been second to none in texture and second to Egyptian only in length of fiber.

22. Temporary packing shed of the Di Giorgio Farms Company.

This map, drawn by Dorothy Nourse, was printed in the May 29, 1922 edition of The Arvin Booster. Courtesy of Phil Krauter.

Arvin Historical Society, and some of her early 1900s photographs are included in this book. (Courtesy of Don Burkett.)

In 1923, Southern Pacific laid a rail line in Arvin (pictured above). The Arvin spur line ran off the Southern Pacific track. Arthur J. McFadden laid a connecting rail line in Lamont. The connection was instrumental in setting Arvin up to compete in outside markets. The railroad tracks are visible in the 1946 photograph of Main Street below. At that time, the population of Arvin was approximately 4,042, and the business district was booming. In the 1940s, Arvin had, among other businesses, a bakery, beauty shop, concrete works, drive-in, hospital, pool hall, cotton gin, dentist, fire department, and theater. (Above, courtesy of the Arvin Historical Society; below, courtesy of Don Burkett.)

At over 6,900 feet in elevation, Bear Mountain (pictured above) dominates the view of the Tehachapi Mountains from Arvin. One cannot help but admire its splendor in every season. In spring the vibrant colors of wildflowers bring it to life, animating it with accents of orange, white, and purple. In summer and fall, it is golden, and occasional light snow covers it in the winter. The photograph below of downtown Arvin shows Bear Mountain towering over the town in 1948. (Above, courtesy of Mary Durham; below, courtesy of Don Burkett.)

From 1937 to 1941, the West Coast Soaring Championships took place at the Arvin-Sierra Gliderport on Tejon Ranch near White Wolf Grade. The public could enjoy watching famous pilots soar above. Woody Brown flew his sailplane *Thunderbird* from Arvin to Bakersfield in April 1939. It became the most important glider port in California. It was shut down during World War II. Pictured above are Phil Krauter (second from right) with Virginia Swanson and two unidentified women from Arvin enjoying the glider meet sponsored by the Southern California Soaring Association. (Both, courtesy of Don Burkett.)

The Arvin Lions Club was established in March 1939. Clyde A. Patterson was a charter member and the first president of the club. From its inception, the club's mission was to serve the community. Members organized numerous events including a donkey basketball game to raise scholarship money for Arvin High School students. The Lions Club has a tradition of holding a speech contest in which seniors compete for a chance to win a scholarship. In 1955, the winners were Margaret Mitchell, Judy Mitchell, and Pat Leary. Ken Loumaugh presents the awards to the students as vice principal Ed DeMello observes. (Courtesy of Don Burkett.)

A typical scene in 1940s Arvin is captured in this photograph of John Plott and his dog Smitty near Durham Street and Walnut Drive. The walnut tree in the background is said to be the street's namesake. Local merchants operated a fruit stand out of the building on the left. (Courtesy of Don Burkett.)

In the 1943 photograph above, Minnie May Young and her son James Clark Young, the author of this book's foreword, are walking near the corner of Laurel and Stockton Street. Willet's Labor Camp can be spotted in the background. The Young family was originally from Arkansas. On their journey west they temporarily settled in Oklahoma and Texas. James Young was born in Shamrock, Texas. His family arrived in California in 1939 and settled in Arvin. James dedicated his life to serving the community. He and his wife, Ruth, live in Arvin. Pictured below from left to right are Ruben Ramirez (an Arvin High School wrestling coach), James Young, and former California governor Pat Brown in 1975. (Above, courtesy of the Arvin Historical Society; below, courtesy of James C. Young.)

The Arvin Women's Club was established around the 1950s. Members worked collaboratively and diligently to advance causes that benefited the community. In 1954, the Women's Club float "Going Home for Christmas" took first place at the Annual Christmas parade. Below, members participate in the ground-breaking ceremony of the Arvin Women's Club building in the early 1950s. It was erected on the corner of Haven Drive and South A Street. (Above, courtesy of Don Burkett; below, courtesy of the Arvin Historical Society.)

On the morning of July 21, 1952, a fatal 7.5-magnitude earthquake struck Kern County. The tremor was one of the most powerful in California's history. It was felt across 160,000 square miles and shook up the Arvin, Lamont, and Weedpatch area. Many buildings, especially those made of brick, sustained major structural damage and several were later demolished. The damage to businesses on Main Street is visible in these photographs. Some residents slept outdoors for weeks after the earthquake while aftershocks persisted. (Both, courtesy of W.C. Stampes.)

Oscar and Johnnie Mae Sanders are pictured above around 1956 with their cousin David Morgan and Pauline Morgan. The Sanders arrived in Arvin in 1942. Their daughter Joycene (pictured at right at the age of 12) married Bill Tarver, and they raised six children in Arvin. Joycene and Bill organized an annual Arvin Easter egg hunt. They, along with other community members and businesses, bought, boiled, colored, and hid 7,000 eggs for the fifth annual egg hunt in the mid-1970s. Their son Tim Tarver served as the mayor of Arvin, and their daughter Charlene is an educator in the community. (Both, courtesy of Charlene Tarver.)

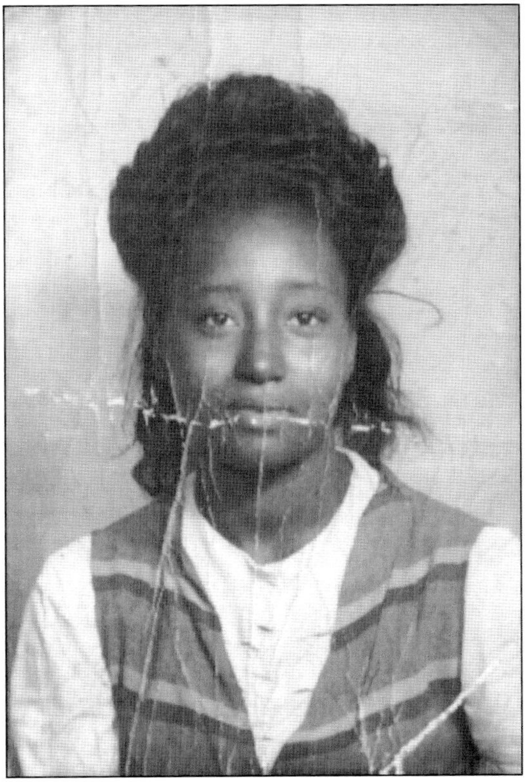

Arvin has a long tradition of participating in and earning awards at the Kern County Fair. The fair provided residents an opportunity to creatively showcase the best elements of Arvin. Pictured are volunteers working the Arvin booth at the Kern County Fair in September 1954. (Courtesy of Don Burkett.)

In 1942, the Kern County Fire Station was located on A Street. It was later moved to Campus Drive. The first police station was located at the Texaco service station on Main Street. A new police station was built on Campus Drive (pictured around 1950). Arvin City Hall's city council chambers and administrative offices were added later. (Courtesy of Don Burkett.)

On December 21, 1960, after decades of functioning as an unincorporated community, Arvin officially became a city. The measure passed with a majority of votes in favor of incorporation. Community leaders, including Elmer C. Smotherman, Judge Joe Collins, Larry Austin, Phil Krauter, supervisor John Holt, Leroy Jackson, state senator Walter Stiern, Dave Head, Jack Van Zant, and county clerk Vera K. Gibson gathered for the ribbon-cutting ceremony to celebrate the widening of Bear Mountain Boulevard in 1970. The sign reads, "Garden in the Sun," which is still the city's logo. (Both, courtesy of Don Burkett.)

The wildflowers that graced the hills surrounding Arvin were a natural phenomenon that attracted admirers from near and far. Lupines, owl's clovers, California poppies, and other flowers made up the colorful landscape. The quantity of wildflowers was determined by the rainfall in the spring each year. The wind storm of 1977 removed 25 million tons of soil from the area. After the storm, the wildflowers did not bloom in as large quantities as they had in the golden years. (Courtesy of the Arvin Historical Society.)

On December 20–21, 1977, one of California's worst weather events of the century struck the area. High- and low-pressure systems caused blinding 90-mile-per-hour winds and gusts that reached 192 miles per hour. Eyewitnesses described apocalyptic conditions in which the sun was blocked and property destroyed. The storm caused $34 million in damage and hit the agricultural industry at its roots. Mayor Frank Gipson urgently requested that Gov. Edmund G. Brown Jr. declare the city in a state of emergency, and the request was eventually granted. Principal Jack Schulze and the Red Cross opened a relief center at Arvin High School to house the 400 residents who were forced to evacuate their homes. More than 100 city, state, and federal workers joined residents in the cleanup efforts. (Courtesy of the Arvin Historical Society.)

Above, from left to right, Juanita Stalcup, Pera Richardson, Evelyn Stalcup, and an unidentified woman are surrounded by wildflowers in a field near Arvin in the 1940s. The Arvin Wildflower Festival (below) was established in the 1930s. It was a special time for residents to gather and admire poppies, lupines, and owl's clovers, among other flowers. After the 1977 windstorm, which removed topsoil that helped the wildflowers to thrive, the proceeds from the festival were used to reseed the hills so that the flowers would grow abundantly once again. In the 1980s and 1990s, the festival included booths, music, and a parade. The Arvin Chamber of Commerce has traditionally been responsible for coordinating the festival. Presently, it is held at Smotherman Park in April. (Above, courtesy of Laverne Wernli; below, courtesy of the Arvin Historical Society.)

Earthquakes, floods, and windstorms are common in the area. These photographs illustrate the damage done by the 1932 flood. After floods in the 1930s and 1940s, farmers built an east-west berm called the Tamarisk Tree Line. It protected Arvin from flooding but sent the water of Caliente Creek down a narrow channel toward Lamont, causing flooding during periods of heavy rainstorms. (Both, courtesy of the Arvin Historical Society.)

The Kern County Lamont Branch Library was established in the 1930s. A branch opened in 1952 and 1974. A new building was opened on August 22, 1996, at 8304 Segrue Road next to Lamont Park. The library has always been a welcoming place for individuals and families. The Kern County sheriff's substation and court and a community center were also located near the park. On September 16, 1947, a post office was established in Lamont. Barbara L. Plymale served as the postmaster. A new post office was dedicated in 1960. (Courtesy of the Kern County Library.)

The area is well known for its Mediterranean climate, with hot, dry summers and mild winters. Although the climate is good for farming, no one can entirely escape the oppressive heat of the summer months. Swimming in canals and small reservoirs provided some relief from the heat. Here, the White family is pictured at a reservoir in the area. (Courtesy of the Dust Bowl Foundation.)

Life was not easy for migrants in search of a better life. With little to no money, they camped wherever they could and labored in the fields or anywhere else they could find work. Some families were able to purchase land to construct humble homes. Pictured is a small community made up of newcomers in Lamont in the 1940s. (Photograph by Dorothea Lange, courtesy of the National Archives.)

The first Lamont Fall Festival and Parade took place in 1947. Actor Scotty Beckett was the grand marshal and is pictured riding down Main Street. The festival consisted of a parade, rodeo, and carnival. It attracted people from near and far, reaching the thousands in 1954. The proceeds paid for the Lamont Junior Baseball Association (JBA) baseball diamonds. The JBA began in June 1957. The baseball diamond is still at Lamont Park, where a sign reads, "Home of the Lamont J.B.A." Behind the crowd, Carlton's service station, Rhodes Market, and Douglas gas station are visible. (Courtesy of the Kern County Museum.)

Lamont has always had a large population of agricultural workers. The Neal, McCoy, and Witheam families lived in Lamont and worked in agriculture like many other families. Their children, including David Neal, Gene Witheam, Bud Witheam, Dale Witheam, and Elton Neal, are pictured above on Kearney Street in the early 1950s. The families lived in homes like the ones seen in these photographs. Pictured below from left to right are Donald McCoy, Elton Neal, Louise McCoy, Ola Neal, Labetta Neal, Earlene McCoy, and David Neal at 325 Kearney Avenue. (Both, courtesy of Labetta Glenn.)

Migrant families came from all over the United States, but many came from the southern plains states. Many settled in temporary housing, and some eventually made the decision to move to Lamont permanently. Atwood and Vergie Risner, originally from Oklahoma, married and lived at the Government Camp with their family starting in 1945. Pictured above are two of their children, Kendell Risner and Jimmy Phillips, outside their home at the Government Camp. In 1953, they moved into a home of their own on Santa Ana Street in Lamont. Jimmy Phillips, Sharon (Risner) Garrison, and Carl Pearson are pictured in front of that home in 1953. Jimmy Phillips became a barber and talented musician who played for Buck Owens and Merle Haggard. (Both, courtesy of the Dust Bowl Foundation.)

Three

SCHOOLS

In 1913, the Bear Mountain School District was created, and the first school (pictured) was erected. Bear Mountain School was named after the mountain overlooking the community. It was a two-room, wooden structure that cost about $4,000 to construct. It was located on Third Avenue between B and C Streets and was a hub of cultural life in the town. On March 8, 1917, the name of the district was changed to Arvin School District. The change from Bear Mountain School to Arvin School may have come after Arvin became the official name of the town. (Courtesy of the Arvin Historical Society.)

Arvin Grammar School students pose with their teacher in 1924. The well-dressed group reflects the fashion of the time. The teacher was Mrs. Ray, and the students are from the Cobb, Hudson, Krauter, Arvizu, Mitchell, Stamps, Osner, and Short families. (Courtesy of Don Burkett.)

Pictured above are students lined up outside of Arvin School in 1919. Mattie B. Adams is believed to have been the first teacher at Arvin School. The first students were from the Shoemaker, Davise, Tucker, Adams, and Heard families. By 1922, the student population continuously grew, so the school hired two additional teachers and added an extra room to accommodate the students. Ralph Haven, J.D. Tucker, and George Richardson served as the trustees of the school district. Pictured below is Arvin's 1926–1927 first-grade class. (Above, courtesy of Arvin Historical Society; below, courtesy of Mildred Blackburn.)

An increase in the student population in the area was seen starting in the 1920s. Arvin schoolchildren are pictured above in 1929. An Arvin School float is seen below riding down the King Cotton Parade route in Bakersfield in 1920. (Above, courtesy of Mildred Blackburn; below, photograph by Dorothy Nourse, courtesy of Don Burkett.)

A second Arvin School was constructed in 1928. The new brick school consisted of two rooms, but additional classrooms were added over time. Gorden Ives and Phil Krauter are seen at right raising the flag in 1931 during the annual playday, a gathering of schools from Arvin, Vineland, and Lamont. The photograph below captures a rare sighting of Arvin School dusted in a thin blanket of snow. (Right, courtesy of Don Burkett; below, courtesy of the Arvin Historical Society.)

Above, Grandville Hendrix (left) and Westley Monroe Young stand in front of an Arvin School District bus in 1948. Young began working as a bus driver and custodian for the school district in 1944. In 1949, the district became the Arvin Union School District. Below, staff members including Lawrence Wernli (standing second from left) and Archie Weeks, Henry Porterfield, Otis Buchanan, Westley M. Young (first row, fourth from left), Fred Vietti, and others are pictured around the 1950s. (Above, courtesy of James C. Young; below, courtesy of Laverne Wernli.)

Not far from Arvin on the San Sebastian Indian Reservation was the Indian School, which served fewer than 20 students since its founding in 1920. The Indian School District joined with the Arvin School District in 1949, and the merger led to the creation of the Arvin Union School District. The district also operated a nearby elementary school named Meridian School until it closed in 1974. Pictured are students of the district. (Above, courtesy of Mildred Blackburn; below, courtesy of Don Burkett.)

Constructed in 1938, Haven Drive became the second school in Arvin. Initially, it served elementary students, but in subsequent years it only served seventh- and eighth-grade students. Students are pictured above dressed sharply for what appears to be a graduation ceremony. Below is a group of students around 1954. (Courtesy of Don Burkett.)

In 1939, the district gained over 100 square miles as a result of annexations ordered by the Kern County Board of Supervisors, providing room for growth needed due to the influx of migrants. In a period of 10 years from 1938 to 1948, the average daily attendance jumped from 550 to 1,283. Pictured are seventh graders at Haven Drive in 1941. (Courtesy of Don Burkett.)

As the population increased, the Arvin Union School District built new schools. In 1960, Sierra Vista Elementary School opened its doors. Bear Mountain Elementary School followed in 1992, and El Camino Real Elementary School was built in 2007. Here, students and staff members of

the Arvin Union School District gather for a photograph in April 1950. (Courtesy of the Dust Bowl Foundation.)

The Kern County Board of Supervisors established Rockpile School on February 6, 1897. The name was influenced by a nearby geographical formation. There were 22 students at the time, and the teacher was Ella Ripley. It was closed from 1905 to 1908 because of low enrollment. The building pictured above was a gathering place for the community, with dances on Saturday nights and church services on Sundays. The original building was destroyed in a fire in 1928 but later rebuilt. The school experienced growth in the 1930s with enrollment at 204 during the 1937–1938 school year. Pictured below is a second-grade class in 1937. Joseph Di Giorgio made a gift of $150,000 and 40 acres of land to the district on Christmas Eve 1945, and the school's name was changed to Di Giorgio School the following year. (Both, courtesy of Don Burkett.)

Mt. View School was formed on March 5, 1894. The original building was less than a mile east of the present building on Weedpatch Highway. Pictured are students and staff in 1898. James M. Brooks and Georgia Green were two of the early teachers. May Stork taught about 17 students the first year, and in 1911, Lelia Wells taught 22 students. In 1917, the district moved the school to its present location. Marian J. Pruett worked as the school's first bus driver. On July 12, 1960, the district changed its name to Lamont School District. (Courtesy of the Kern County Museum.)

Local schools experienced an increase in student enrollment beginning in the 1930s. Mt. View School had about 154 students by 1935. Ten years later, the district's enrollment exceeded 500, and it was over 1,200 by 1954. The population continued to grow for decades. The district opened Lamont School in 1939 and Myrtle Avenue School on January 3, 1956. In 1967, the district opened Alicante School. Pictured above is Mt. View School in 1926, and below is a fourth-grade class in 1945. (Above, courtesy of Kern County Museum; below, courtesy of the Dust Bowl Foundation.)

As the first school in the Arvin and Lamont area, Vineland School was established May 9, 1890. The one-room school was located at the A.N. Towne Ranch. During the first year, teacher Clara Day taught about 14 students in eight grades. In 1893, a wooden two-story schoolhouse was built (pictured above in 1915). On Saturdays, community members gathered for dances on the second floor. Roy and Opal Harper played the violin and piano, respectively. On Sundays, residents participated in jackrabbit drives. Rev. George Goodell was the first minister of the church, and served other nearby communities, hosting Sunday school and church services at the school. Photographic evidence suggests that the two-story schoolhouse was demolished and the one-story school building next to it (pictured below) was expanded by 1928. The school was damaged by the 1952 earthquake, and new buildings were constructed from 1952 to 1957. The historic bell that was used at two of the previous schools was dedicated on May 30, 1970, at the present-day Vineland School campus. (Above, courtesy of Kern County Museum; below, courtesy of the Arvin Historical Society.)

In the 1930s, the district experienced a growth in student population, owing largely to the influx of migrants from the southern plains states. The number of students was under 40 in 1920 and over 300 by 1940. By 1970, there were 700 students. Pictured here are Vineland students and staff in the 1930s. (Above, courtesy of the Arvin Historical Society; below, courtesy of Vineland School District.)

Many of the children who attended Sunset School lived at the Arvin Migratory Labor Camp, which was in operation by 1936. Migrant children first began attending Vineland School, the nearest school to the camp. According to Peter Bancroft, the small school district experienced overcrowding and financial strain. The migrant students were not welcome at Vineland School and faced discrimination. By the late 1930s, the federal government established the Arvin Federal Emergency (or Migratory) School. (Courtesy of the Dust Bowl Foundation.)

In January 1939, Leo Hart began his tenure as Kern County superintendent of education. Recognizing the educational needs and lack of support for migrant children, Hart asked the Vineland School District School Board for permission to create a school. The school board approved the request, and a school was developed on a 10-acre plot next to the camp. According to Hart, he made an effort to hire the best teachers with an interest in teaching migrant children. When the school opened its doors, it claimed an enrollment of 125. In the beginning, the school lacked toilets, water, and desks, and classroom sizes ranged from 30 to 60, but improvements were made over time. Hart found a way to add a cafeteria, vegetable gardens, and pens in which chickens, sheep, pigs, and cows were raised. The curriculum was expanded to include typewriting, sewing, carpentry, cosmetics, construction, and other skills. The construction of a swimming pool allowed students to put their skills into action. (Courtesy of the Dust Bowl Foundation.)

Eugene Burmeister wrote that the Arvin Federal Emergency School was discontinued in 1943 and replaced by Sunset Elementary School. Leo Hart was told by a state official that emergency schools could only be in operation for five years. In 1944, Peter Bancroft was hired as principal of the school and later served as the superintendent of the Vineland School District. Bancroft helped make Sunset Elementary School part of the Vineland School District. The district acquired the property in 1947 from the federal government, and a new school building was erected on Sunset Avenue. Pictured are Ray Shelton and other students of Sunset School in the late 1940s. (Courtesy of the Dust Bowl Foundation.)

In the 1950s, an aviation class was started at Sunset Elementary School. Peter Bancroft acquired a C-46 and other surplus airplanes (pictured) from the US government, and students were taught aircraft mechanics. Instructors taught some of the lessons inside the C-46. Students who maintained good grades were rewarded by being allowed to taxi the aircraft down a runway. In December 1950, Capt. Charles "Chuck" Yeager, an Air Force pilot famously known for breaking the sound barrier in 1947, visited Sunset Elementary School. Following Captain Yeager's visit, the district took students on a field trip to Edwards Air Force Base. (Courtesy of the Dust Bowl Foundation.)

Until 1949, students in the Arvin, Lamont, and Weedpatch area attended Kern County High School, renamed Bakersfield High School in 1945. Over the course of a decade, Arvin High School would go from an idea to a reality. In 1941, the Kern High School District Board of Trustees purchased 40 acres of land for a new high school. According to Don Burkett, the land was purchased from A.N. George and was leased to Hugh Jewett until the school was constructed. Architect Ernest L. McCoy designed the building, and the plans were approved by the state in 1948. Guy E. Hall secured the contract to build the first segment of the school. Pictured are members of the Arvin High School community celebrating the ground-breaking ceremony in 1948. (Both, courtesy of Don Burkett.)

Hundreds of crew members laid the hallmark brick, drilled the well, erected the 100-foot water tower, and put finishing touches on the new school. A grand 980-seat auditorium, which was later named after Jack O. Schulze, a beloved Arvin High principal, was also constructed. The original construction estimate was $2.6 million. Pictured are students Joe Zaragoza (left, associated with the Zaragoza Market in Weedpatch) and Henry Rangel playing horseshoes in front of Arvin High while it was still under construction. (Courtesy of Mary Durham.)

Arvin High School opened its doors to nearly 600 students on September 12, 1949 (above). The 80-acre campus included a 40-acre farm. Principal Clyde Dawald led a team of 29 teachers and staff members. There was no office or cafeteria the first year. Principal Dawald worked from Bakersfield High School, and students ate along the curb during lunchtime. Students and staff members are pictured below. (Both, courtesy of Don Burkett.)

Since its inception, Arvin High offered numerous academic and extracurricular opportunities. Core classes, coupled with programs designed to help students connect knowledge and skills to the real world, have made Arvin High shine. Programs including Future Farmers of America (pictured above), choir (pictured below around the 1950s), and student government were established early on and are still active today. (Both, courtesy of Don Burkett.)

Arvin High athletic teams began competing in 1949. The warriors were selected as the mascot, which was changed to the bears in 1950. Red and white became the official school colors. Above is Arvin's first football team playing at Sunset School. From left to right are (first row) Glen Bailey, Lorn Best, Joe Coleman, Arthur Ingle, John Rutledge, Bruce Polk, and Ray Robinson; (second row) Bill Riley, Jerry Pool, Wayland Oakes, and Junior Watts. The football team was coached by the legendary Frank Barle, whom the stadium is named after. Introduced by Barle, the common offensive formation for the team was the single wing. Pictured below is Arvin's football team in the 1960s coached by Don Burkett, a local historian, writer, and teacher at Arvin High. (Both, courtesy of Don Burkett.)

The Arvin High Girls Athletic Association (GAA) enabled female students to play basketball, field hockey, softball, cross country, and more against each other, but tennis was the only competitive sport offered until Title IX in 1972. Thereafter, a full array of female sports programs was offered. Two highly esteemed tennis coaches were Caroline Leary and Linda Shepard. (Courtesy of Don Burkett.)

Athletic programs at Arvin benefit greatly from alumni groups that provide support in various ways. The Arvin Boosters Club is a well-established network that provides support, including fundraising. The Arvin High Athletic Hall of Fame celebrates talented former athletes. Pictured here from left to right are esteemed coaches Charles "Chuck" Chamberlin, Billy Satterfield, and Grant Hamilton on the field in the 1970s. (Courtesy of Don Burkett.)

The Arvin High students who matriculated the year it opened its doors were called "the 49ers." The school's first graduating class walked across the stage in 1952. The first yearbook, called *Praeterita*, was published in 1950, and the student newspaper was called the *Bear Facts*. Pictured here is the Arvin High band in 1965. Years later, it became the Crimson Bear Brigade. (Courtesy of the Arvin Historical Society.)

The Arvin High Alumni Association has been crucial for the advancement of the school and students. Every year, the alumni association raises scholarship money to benefit deserving seniors. Members truly embody the phrase "once a bear, always a bear." Pictured at left are Arvin faculty members at a club game scholarship benefit in 1953. Arvin High continues to be a source of pride in Arvin, Lamont, and Weedpatch. (Left, courtesy of Don Burkett; below, courtesy of the Arvin Historical Society.)

Four

FAITH

In 1912, community members began attending church services at the home of J.D. Tucker. The following year, the newly constructed Bear Mountain School was used for Sunday school. The church was organized on June 17, 1914, and consisted of Methodists and Baptists. Together, they decided to become part of the Congregational denomination. Charter members included J.D. and Annie Tucker, Ralph and Effa Haven, Pearly Gregory, Mrs. Charles Adams, and a Mr. Cameron. The church was incorporated on May 26, 1919, as the Arvin Union Congregational Church. (Courtesy of the Arvin Historical Society.)

George Clark was the first minister of what became the Arvin Union Congregational Church. The parsonage was built on Main Street in 1919 on land donated by Orange Belt Farms. Its construction cost $900, and it served as the home of Reverend Peebles and his family, who began serving in October 1918. Rev. Nathan Packard is seen above next to the parsonage in 1922 and at left with his family in 1924. He was a minister from 1922 to 1929 and again from 1932 to 1935. (Above, courtesy of the Arvin Historical Society; left, courtesy of Don Burkett.)

Sunday school attendees gathered for this photograph in 1917. The Arvin Union Congregational Church used the schoolhouse until May 1923, when the construction of a new building began. The lot next to the parsonage was donated to the church by the T.H. Derby family of Bakersfield, and local architect Clinton Nourse drew the plans as a labor of love. The cost of construction was approximately $10,500. The church was dedicated on October 24, 1924. According to Eugene Burmeister, it was used by community members for important events such as weddings, funerals, and conferences. (Courtesy of Don Burkett.)

The 7.5-magnitude earthquake of 1952 damaged the church, but it was repaired. In the 1960s, a Mr. Jewett donated land at Campus Drive and Varsity Road for a new church. Membership was in the 200s in the 1950s but dwindled thereafter. Mabel Krauter remembered that there was tension between the "farm-oriented" congregants and supporters of the farm labor movement in the 1960s, and the minster relocated to Fresno. Pictured below are members at the church's golden anniversary celebration in 1964. The church made the decision to tear down the old original building in 1971, and in 1977, the mortgage for the new church was paid off. In July 2014, Arvin Union Congregational became St. John's Valley of Faith, part of the St. John's Lutheran Church of Bakersfield and the Lutheran Church–Missouri Synod. (Above, courtesy of the Arvin Historical Society; below, courtesy of Don Burkett.)

In 1920, the Ladies Aid Society was organized at the home of Birdie Heard. The group raised $100 for a future church building. Mable Krauter noted that the women of the church recognized and met the needs of the church throughout its history. Pictured at right from left to right are Ferrol (Heard) Combs, Anabel Krauter, Myrtis Krauter, and Mable Krauter in 1919. Ferrol and Mabel actively preserved the history of Arvin and the Arvin Union Congregational Church. Pictured below are Mabel Krauter and her Sunday school class in 1950. (Right, courtesy of Don Burkett; below, courtesy of the Arvin Historical Society.)

In 1926, the Church of the Nazarene, Arvin's second church and parsonage, was established on B Street at the home of the pastor. Around 1940, a building was constructed on Stockton and Orange Streets. In 1958, a new church was purchased on Arvin Street (pictured below). In 1968, the church relocated to Hill Street, where it remains today. In 2002, it became a Spanish language church, which is presently active in Arvin. (Above, courtesy of Don Burkett; below, courtesy of James C. Young.)

Arvin experienced a growth in churches of various denominations after the 1930s. Bright Hope Baptist Church on Santa Rosa Street and Church of God in Christ on C Street are thriving African American churches that have served the community since the 1950s. Congregants of the Church of God in Christ, pastored by N. Duffy, came together for this photograph. Other churches of the era included Freewill Baptist, Calvary Baptist, First Baptist, and Arvin Adventist. (Courtesy of Charlene Tarver.)

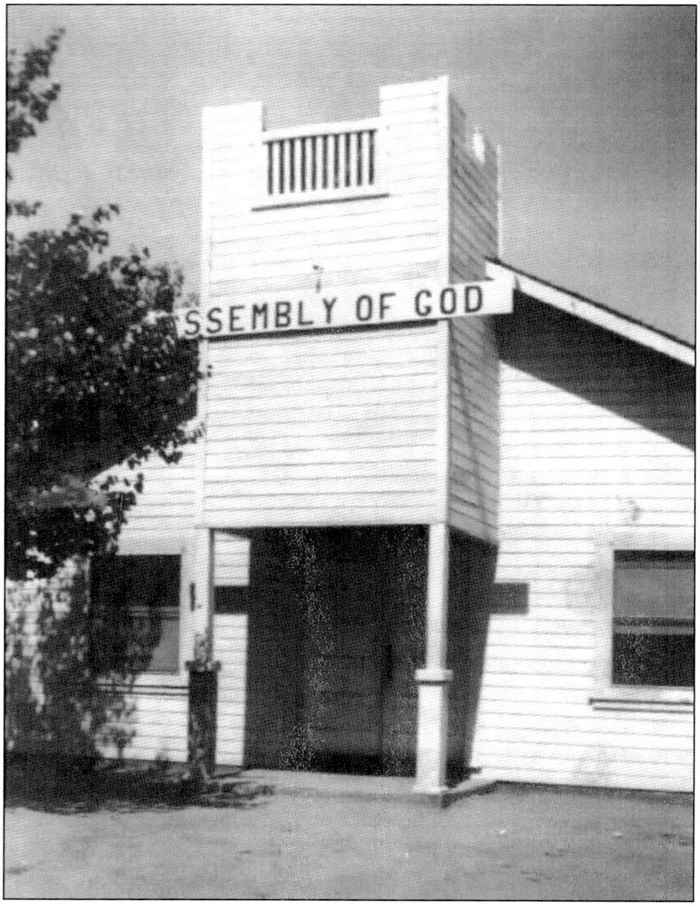

Mabel Jobe, who served the Assembly of God church for over 65 years, wrote that Sister Drake started the Assembly of God church when she led the first service under a grape arbor. Worshipers met in various homes until Frank Robles took on the role of pastor of the congregation. In 1930, the first church building was erected at the corner of B and Fourth Streets (pictured at left in 1936). Rev. Cynthia Roden and her family pastored the church at that time. A parsonage was built in the 1950s on Hill Street. Rev. Ben Sapp pastored from 1963 to 1973, during which time the building was remodeled, and a new parsonage was built on Orchard Drive. Below, a group of children pose for a Mother's Day photograph in 1939. (Both, courtesy of Laverne Wernli.)

In 1941, Rev. Dwight Brown and his family began pastoring the Assembly of God church. A new building was constructed in 1950 on the corner of Hill and Tucker Streets. Congregants, including Albert Jobe, constructed the church in a labor of love. Above, the congregation poses in front of the new building in 1951. The church has been active in the community since its early years. The church's eye-catching floats were proudly displayed at Arvin's annual Christmas parades. In 1954, the float pictured below won the trophy. (Both, courtesy of Laverne Wernli.)

The Easter sunrise service began in 1927 on White Wolf Grade east of Arvin. An account notes that Lydia Yaussy compared the terrain to Calvary, where Jesus was crucified. A wooden cross was placed in the granite rock overlooking Arvin. In the 1930s, metal from an oilfield pipe was used to replace the wooden cross. It was later replaced by a metal cross made at E.O. Mitchell's shop. Members of the Bear Mountain Ministerial Association handled the preparations. The service at the cross is a yearly tradition for many Arvin residents. Tejon Ranch owns the land and permits the service for free. The cross is seen at left in a 1950 photograph of Alfed Joe McCoy and in the distance below. (Left, courtesy of Labetta Glenn; below, courtesy of the Arvin Historical Society.)

Padre Francisco Garces passed through the area in 1776, planting the seeds of Catholicism. The fathers assigned to the area set out to convert Tejon Indians. Pictured is a Christian church on the Indian reservation at Tejon Ranch, possibly between 1888 and 1900. (Courtesy of the Library of Congress.)

St. Thomas the Apostle Catholic Church began as a mission of Saint Joseph Catholic Church of Bakersfield, which was erected in 1907 and was at the time part of the Roman Catholic Diocese of Monterey–Los Angeles. In the mid-1930s, Fr. A.C. Stuhlmann (pictured) would hold a monthly private mass in a home in Arvin. He went on to serve as the first pastor of the church from 1939 to 1940. (Courtesy of the Roman Catholic Diocese of Fresno.)

In June 1938, the construction of St. Thomas the Apostle Catholic Church began (pictured above). The Mission Revival–style adobe building was constructed on five acres of land donated by Thomas H. and Elizabeth Derby in 1936. Joseph Di Giorgio, Peter Cattani, and Dana Hogan provided financial assistance for the completion of the building. Parishioners donated their time and labor toward its construction. The final product is pictured at left in 1939. (Both, courtesy of the Roman Catholic Diocese of Fresno.)

The clergy of the St. Thomas the Apostle Catholic Church held the first mass and dedication ceremony on November 12, 1939, and the building was dedicated on July 27, 1941. Hundreds of people attended the dedication officiated by Rev. Philip G. Scher, Bishop of the Monterey-Fresno Diocese. Two special guests were Chief Juan Losada, a Tejon Indian whose ancestors accompanied Father Garces to the site in 1776, and Damon Caesar Larios, whose family had lived in California for seven generations. A group of children from the Tejon Indian Reservation and descendants of early Spanish settlers participated in the service. A statue of Fr. Francisco Garces was unveiled, and the Rancho Grande orchestra of Di Giorgio composed of Gavino Rangel, Juan Herrera, Ponciano Pena, Mariano Rangel, and Luis Hernandez played afterward. Pictured is the interior of the church. (Courtesy of the Roman Catholic Diocese of Fresno.)

The 1952 earthquake that struck the area inflicted structural damage on St. Thomas the Apostle Catholic Church. It was temporarily closed because of the destruction and potential danger. The cost of repairs was estimated at $50,000. Pictured above is the updated and retrofitted church. The church hosted *jamaicas* (festivals), at which community members could fellowship together over food, music, and dancing. Arvin resident and community leader Toni Pichardo recalls attending the jamaicas. She lived on Langford and later Monroe Street in the 1960s. Other Mexican families, a majority of whom were Catholics, lived in the neighborhood. (Courtesy of the Roman Catholic Diocese of Fresno.)

Dorothea Lange captured migrant laborers assembled to collect California State Relief Administration pay in the 1930s. She noted that most of the men in line were living in "shacktown" communities in the Arvin area. The building in the photograph was used for various purposes, including meetings and Church of Christ services. (Photograph by Dorothea Lange; courtesy of National Archives.)

Catholic families living at the Di Giorgio Camp did not have to go far to attend mass. In the 1930s, Fr. A.C. Stuhlmann held a monthly mass at the Di Giorgio Camp. Jesus Lozano was the catechist. Believers in this image were captured participating in an open-air mass at Di Giorgio Camp. (Courtesy of the Roman Catholic Diocese of Fresno.)

Prior to the migration of the 1930s, the majority of the churches were Mainline Protestant. Historians, however, have noted that the arrival of Dust Bowl migrants radically changed the religious landscape of the area. The migrants brought with them southern religious folkways of Pentecostal and Southern Baptist churches. Through the years, settlers and migrants spread their faith in the area, as seen in the Lamont Assembly of God Church photograph above and the baptism below. Mexican Pentecostals established a church in Lamont in the early 1950s. In 1962, the *Bakersfield Californian* listed the following churches in Lamont: Community Methodist Church on Main Street, First Assembly of God on Kearney Street, North Lamont Assembly of God on Myrtle and Paradise, Harmony Baptist Church on Santa Paula and Wharton Streets, New Bethel Missionary Baptist Church on Paradise and Velma, Lamont First Southern Baptist Church, Church of Christ on Gail Marie Drive, General Assembly of Church of Jesus on Kearney and San Diego, Shepherd of the Valley Lutheran Church on Myrtle Avenue, and Pentecostal Holiness Church on Velma and Bonita streets. (Both, courtesy of the Dust Bowl Foundation.)

Since the 1930s, the Lamont area experienced a growth in population, and the demand for a Catholic church increased. Prior to the construction of a church, Fr. Arturo Liebranz, O.F.M., set up a mobile chapel on the property of Miguel Valenzuela. In the early 1960s, the Roman Catholic Diocese of Monterey-Fresno selected Fr. Placido Lanz, O.A.R. (pictured at left), to begin the Catholic church in Lamont. He was responsible for securing a site for the new church and raising funds to construct it. Nine acres of land were purchased in 1962 for $20,000. It is believed that there were about 75 families, a majority of which were Mexican. The sisters of the church cooked tamales to help raise money for the construction of the church. During the year of construction, mass was held at the Village Theater at the corner of Main Street and Segrue Road. The St. Augustine Church was constructed in 1963. In the 1970s, the church held *jamaicas* in the evenings. They were popular events for the whole community to enjoy. They included food booths, games, *lotería* (Mexican bingo), live performances, and dances. (Both, courtesy of the Roman Catholic Diocese of Fresno.)

Five

Businesses and Agriculture

On November 1, 1917, A. Tim Staples opened the Arvin Store (pictured). Staples sold groceries and later added general merchandise. The Arvin Store housed the post office, public library, and public weight scales. Resident Lawrence Packard is seen in front of the Arvin Store and other businesses in the early 1920s. (Courtesy of the Arvin Historical Society.)

Kern County is known as the breadbasket of the United States. The Kern County Department of Agriculture and Measurement Standards has produced crop reports since 1930. The 1930 report shows that cotton, alfalfa, table grapes, raisins, potatoes, and peas were the most valuable crops that year. The potato crops did particularly well and helped increase awareness about diversified farming. The value of all grapes in Kern County in 1930 was $2,995,060 ($46 million in today's economy). The 2017 report valued all grapes at $1.7 billion. Almonds, including by-products, ranked second at $1.2 billion. This photograph shows the Nourse Vineyards in 1920. (Courtesy of the Arvin Historical Society.)

In 1919, brothers Arnaldo, Manuel, Phil, and Julian Arvizu established the Arvizu Brothers concrete pipe yard business in Arvin. They produced machine-made irrigation pipes and were widely known in Kern County. Manuel, Phil, and Julian built homes in Arvin and purchased 80 acres of land. They successfully grew cotton, expanded their business over time, and were active in the community. Their parents, Domingo and Francesca (Lopez) Arvizu, were originally from Sonora, Mexico, and settled in the Los Angeles area. (Courtesy of the Arvin Historical Society.)

A centerpiece of the Arvin business district was the A.J. Richardson store and service station pictured above. A 1920s version of this store is featured on the cover of this book. The picture below captures the F.E. Peterson service station. Similar to agriculture, oil has been a major industry in the area. (Above, courtesy of Don Burkett; below, courtesy of the Arvin Historical Society.)

Cotton grew to be one of Kern County's most lucrative crops. Farmers in the area increased the planting of cotton from 1917 to 1919, and the need for cotton gins increased. Pictured at left is Arvin's first Pima cotton gin. Below is an industrial gin in 1928. It was originally a long staple gin, and in a few years, it changed to a short or medium staple. The latter was destroyed by a fire. (Left, courtesy of the Arvin Historical Society; below, courtesy of Don Burkett.)

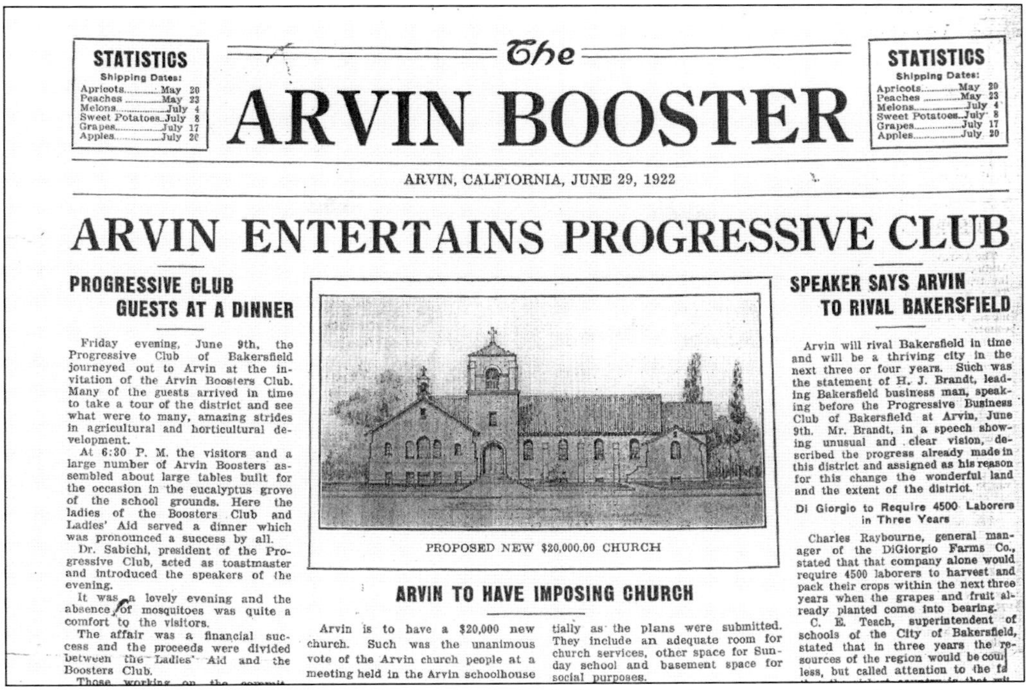

STATISTICS
Shipping Dates:
Apricots..........May 20
Peaches..........May 23
Melons..........July 4
Sweet Potatoes..July 8
Grapes..........July 17
Apples..........July 20

The
ARVIN BOOSTER

ARVIN, CALFIORNIA, JUNE 29, 1922

ARVIN ENTERTAINS PROGRESSIVE CLUB

PROGRESSIVE CLUB GUESTS AT A DINNER

Friday evening, June 9th, the Progressive Club of Bakersfield journeyed out to Arvin at the invitation of the Arvin Boosters Club. Many of the guests arrived in time to take a tour of the district and see what were to many, amazing strides in agricultural and horticultural development.

At 6:30 P. M. the visitors and a large number of Arvin Boosters assembled about large tables built for the occasion in the eucalyptus grove of the school grounds. Here the ladies of the Boosters Club and Ladies' Aid served a dinner which was pronounced a success by all.

Dr. Sabichi, president of the Progressive Club, acted as toastmaster and introduced the speakers of the evening.

It was a lovely evening and the absence of mosquitoes was quite a comfort to the visitors.

The affair was a financial success and the proceeds were divided between the Ladies' Aid and the Boosters Club.

PROPOSED NEW $20,000.00 CHURCH

ARVIN TO HAVE IMPOSING CHURCH

Arvin is to have a $20,000 new church. Such was the unanimous vote of the Arvin church people at a meeting held in the Arvin schoolhouse ... tially as the plans were submitted. They include an adequate room for church services, other space for Sunday school and basement space for social purposes.

SPEAKER SAYS ARVIN TO RIVAL BAKERSFIELD

Arvin will rival Bakersfield in time and will be a thriving city in the next three or four years. Such was the statement of H. J. Brandt, leading Bakersfield business man, speaking before the Progressive Business Club of Bakersfield at Arvin, June 9th. Mr. Brandt, in a speech showing unusual and clear vision, described the progress already made in this district and assigned as his reason for this change the wonderful land and the extent of the district.

Di Giorgio to Require 4500 Laborers in Three Years

Charles Raybourne, general manager of the DiGiorgio Farms Co., stated that that company alone would require 4500 laborers to harvest and pack their crops within the next three years when the grapes and fruit already planted come into bearing.

C. E. Teach, superintendent of schools of the City of Bakersfield, stated that in three years the resources of the region would be coun... less, but called attention to the fa...

The Bear Mountain/Arvin Booster Club published *The Arvin Booster* on a weekly basis in the 1920s. It was originally used to advertise property for sale. Frank D. Reed operated the *Arvin Tiller* from 1939 until his death in 1970. He also purchased the *Arvin Booster* and merged the two publications. His son Frank Wallace Reed, who grew up in Arvin, became his business partner in the 1950s. They purchased the *Lamont Reporter* and published the *Arvin Tiller* and *Lamont Reporter*. Their office was located on Third and A Streets. Wallace operated Reed Print Inc. until he retired in 2018. (Both, courtesy of the Arvin Historical Society.)

THE
ARVIN TILLER
AND BOOSTER

TILLER VOL. 8, NO. 33 — ARVIN, KERN COUNTY, CALIFORNIA, FRIDAY, SEPTEMBER 6, 1946 — BOOSTER VOL. 6, NO. 41

THE GRAPEVINE
FRANK REED

Don't run down your business firm as long as you are receiving your check each week.

* * *

A friend says a woman seems attractive until she says "I done" and "I seen."

* * *

There was the bum with ulcers who asked for a dime for a glass of milk instead of the usual cup of coffee.

* * *

The way some folks anticipate another war, you would think they took real pleasure in the last one.

* * *

The man who courted a girl welder in a mask, was disillusioned when the war was over and she took off the disguise.

* * *

According to a subscriber, it might be sensible to have houses of legislature, one to make new laws and two to repeal them.

* * *

Farming must be getting tough. Bob Tucker is now delivering phone books.

* * *

Di Giorgio School To Enrich Corriculum

The Di Giorgio School District is planning to present an enriched educational program to its estimated 250 pupils for the 1946-47 school term. In addition to the required courses in the fundamental tool subjects, the following offerings will be available to pupils to meet their individual needs and interests. Namely, agriculture, shop, home economics, Spanish, speech correction, art, music and a mobile commercial unit to teach typing and accounting. Visual aids will also play a large part in the instruction process.

School will begin on September 9, with a well balance teaching staff on hand. A full days' program is planned and luncheon will be served to the school children. Parents of pupils entering the first grade should plan to enroll their children during the peliminary registration on September 7, from two to four p. m. First graders must be five years and six months by September 1, 1946. Buses will travel approximately the same routes as last year.

The new teachers who have been employed in the Di Giorgio ...

Arvin War Hero Will Move to Washington

The World At A Glance

Forward Step

A-Bomb's Bull's-Eye

Bouncing Baby

DETROIT, MICH. — Pictured here is Roger Feagan, 14 months, who fell out a third story window in Detroit. After falling out of the window the child was rushed to the hospital where it was found to be unhurt. His father is a reenlisted war veteran. Roger has been walking since he was 9 months old which may explain his ability to fall out of third story windows.

Businessmen's Dance Held at Hall Tonight

Hundreds will attend the Arvin ...

Arvin To Have Booth At County Fair

Arvin will be represented this year with a booth at Kern County's annual fair. The Arvin Businessmen's club will sponsor this exhibit with Del Smith chairman of the committee. Mr. Smith said:

We are extremely anxious that Arvin be well represented and have a good exhibit, and since farm fruits, crops and produce will be the principal products on display, we want the very best that is available for this booth. Anyone having especially nice or large produce should contact Mr. Smith, and make arrangements for delivery and storage so that it will be available when the booth decorating committee is ready to prepare the booth.

"This is another of those activities that are the responsibility of every one and the committee will need the assistance of all of us to make this a display of which we can all be proud, so let's all get together and look for attractive poduce for this exhibit.

FAMILY REUNION

Mr. and Mrs. Asa Canterberry's children gathered at their ...

By 1924, Arvin was a well-established town and home to a growing business scene. Lawrence Nourse and A. Tim Staples helped launch the Bear Mountain Boosters Club in 1921 (renamed Arvin Boosters Club in 1925). The group produced the weekly *Arvin Booster*. In August 1924, the *Booster* reported that Arvin had a school, church, post office, library, railroad service, a main road leading to town, service stations, a hotel and restaurant, and packing sheds. Louis Ward and Elva Bornhauser opened the Arvin Grill (pictured below), the first restaurant and hotel in town, on June 1, 1921. In 1922, the Arvin Mutual Telephone Company was organized. There were three stores and another one being constructed, which meant that the townspeople did not have to travel long distances for basic necessities. (Both, courtesy of the Arvin Historical Society.)

The classic 1925 photograph above provides a snapshot of the area and time. Transporting the Nourse and Staples market-ready cotton is a Ford Model T pickup truck. The bales of cotton were sold for $1 per pound. Alcala and Pima cotton were staple crops in the area. On the lower left side of the advertisement, the name of a prominent Arvin farmer, Robert "Bob" Barlow, can be seen. It is believed that a group of African Americans lived and worked on Barlow's farm. Pictured below is a Nourse Farms truck with Pima cotton ready to be shipped overseas in 1920. (Above, courtesy of Don Burkett; below, courtesy of the Arvin Historical Society.)

The Brick Store, owned by Ralph L. Thayer and Earl O. Mitchell, opened in 1924. A Mr. Weaver sold his share to Mitchell, who later sold it to Thayer. The building later served as a department store, jewelry store, beauty shop, and restaurant. (Both, courtesy of the Arvin Historical Society.)

Austin's, a gas and fountain service store, was one of several stores in Arvin in 1939. It was located across the street from Haven Drive School. Pictured from left to right are (first row) Juanita Crow, Billy Austin, Mrs. Austin, Pauline Austin, and Lee Austin; (second row) Vester Crow, W.D. Austin, and Odelle, Rommie, Dee, and Larry Austin. (Courtesy of Don Burkett.)

The growing demand for entertainment in the community led to the opening of movie theaters. Arvin Theater, the first in town, was on Arvin Street. The theater is pictured burning in 1939. It was reopened for business after undergoing repairs. A new theater named El Rancho opened its doors in 1949 on Bear Mountain Boulevard. James Banducci owned and operated both theaters. By the 1950s, the Arvin Theater started showing Spanish-language movies, including *La Reina Del Mambo* and *Fijate Que Suave*, while El Rancho played *Carson City* and *No Room for the Groom*. (Courtesy of the Kern County Museum.)

In 1950, Mitchells was located at the northwest corner of Sunset Avenue and Comanche Drive (pictured above). Mitchells offered various goods and services for small and large farms. At left, a man is pictured hard at work inside the shop. E.O. Mitchell owned a ranch and served as an Arvin School District trustee. (Both, courtesy of the Arvin Historical Society.)

Bobby Permenter and Millard Finis "Buck" Permenter posed for a photograph in Buck's cotton fields in Arvin. Buck moved to Arvin in 1923. He and his wife, Millie (Jenkins) Permenter, raised their family in Arvin. Buck worked in the oil fields and on a farm before growing potatoes and cotton on his 160-acre farm. He was on the Arvin Union School District Board of Trustees from 1933 to 1939. Their daughter Mildred (Permenter) Blackburn attended the Arvin Grammar School and graduated from Kern County Union School (Bakersfield High School) in 1938. She rode the bus with about 30 students from Arvin to Bakersfield. Later, she earned a college degree and married Vernon Harrison Blackburn. Mildred attended the Congregational church and was a member of the Arvin Women's Club. She still resides in Arvin with her family, and their business, Blackburn Oil Company, is still in operation. (Both, courtesy of Mildred Blackburn.)

By 1950, the population in Arvin exceeded 5,000. The businesses in town met the various needs of residents. The majority of the businesses were located on Third Avenue (Bear Mountain Boulevard). Many flocked to the Circle Dot Drive-in, where beef and beans could be purchased for $1.25. The photograph above shows the front of the Valley Mercantile Company and Sprouse Reitz Co. on Main Street. Below is the Bank of America in 1950. (Both, courtesy of the Arvin Historical Society.)

In 1925, there were several businesses in Lamont including Robert Byer's Barbershop, the Lamont Meat Market, Safeway, Randleman's Richfield Station and Garage, Bert Combs' Garage and Gas Station, and Hazel Waters' Cafe. Wayne and Sarah Peaye are pictured next to Lamont's first barbershop in 1922. Oil rigs were set up in Lamont by 1925. The first producing oil well was drilled in 1933 on a Mt. View field owned by S.E.L Wharton, by Dana Hogan Petroleum Company. (Courtesy of the Arvin Historical Society.)

Lamont enjoyed a thriving business district in the 1950s. Prominent businesses in town included Betty's Dress shop, Lamont Lumber Company, the Lamont Store, C&C Shell station, Fred's Drive-In, C&W Cafe, and Allen's Auto Supply Parts and Accessories. (Courtesy of the Dust Bowl Foundation.)

In the 1950s, the Collins family from Weedpatch held a weekly auction under a tent in Lamont. The auction took place on Wednesday and Sunday afternoons and featured second-hand furniture and other home items. Celebrity names like Bonnie Owens drew in residents who enjoyed country-western entertainment. The Collins family purchased 17 acres and built a shopping center between Hall Road and Gail Marie Drive. Rufeners Drug Store, County Fair Clothing, Country Fair Market, Collins Furniture Store, the post office, and Cornet Store comprised the new shopping center. Joe Collins served as a judge for the Arvin-Lamont Judicial District. (Courtesy of the Dust Bowl Foundation.)

The Lamont Reporter

A WEEKLY NEWSPAPER BELONGING TO ITS SUBSCRIBERS AND AT THEIR SERVICE

E VI — NUMBER 2 LAMONT, CALIFORNIA, THURSDAY, NOVEMBER 11, 1954 5 CENTS PER COPY - $2.50 A

ound and
out Lamont
with Burt Cantor

es Watson spent Friday with Barbara Johnson in ield. Barbara came home her and spent Saturday nd Sunday.

nd Mrs. T. E. Carroll were luncheon guests of Rev rs. Van Cunningham in ield.

'Fox' Turoonji
Hurt When Ca
Crashes Bridg

Aslan "Fox" Turoonjia nown local fruit packer a rintendent of the Arvin Growers packing shed on W Street, was injured ear terday morning when his parently went out of contr ing out 30 feet of railing North Chester bridge. It nose down in the dry river feet below the Californ

The Lamont Reporter made its debut on November 17, 1949. The weekly publication was produced by Roy McDowell. Al Cantor became the publisher and editor in November 1951. Mike and Edward Curtis became the owners in January 1963. It was owned by Al Cantor again before being purchased by Frank D. Reed. He published the newspaper until 1970. His son Frank Wallace Reed operated the business until he retired in 2018. The *Lamont Ledger* was another local weekly publication produced by Tony Reed of Tony Reed Publications from 1971 to 1974. Local historians Eugene Burmeister and Don Burkett, among others, wrote about the history of the area in newspaper columns such as "Looking Back with Burkett." The column featured photographs shared by the public and a caption that recapped the past and present. (Courtesy of the Arvin Historical Society.)

The Lamont Drive-in theater was an entertainment destination. On family night, the fee was $1 per car. In July 1956, residents enjoyed watching movies such as *Backlash*, *The Atomic Man*, *Picnic*, *The Way Out*, *The Barefoot Contessa*, and *Stormy*. In 1956, Village Theater played movies all week. On weekdays, patrons could enjoy watching movies starting at 6:30 p.m., and on Sundays, the doors would open at 12:30 p.m. The movies playing at the time were *Showing Postmark for Danger*, *Indestructible Man*, *The Conqueror*, and *The Living Swamp*. Village Theater was at the corner of Main and Segrue Streets. (Courtesy of the Dust Bowl Foundation.)

In the early years, groceries were delivered by wagon from Bakersfield. Elmer (or Earl) Williams opened a small wood frame store in Weedpatch in 1915. The store was a hub for a number of services. Mail was delivered by mail carrier from Bakersfield to Williams's store. A telephone was available for public use. There was a Weedpatch baseball team, and Williams took them to play other teams out of town. Marion Franklin Parish purchased the store in 1920. Parish was the judge of the 15th Township Justice Court. He added a room to his store that functioned as the court. Parish retired in 1937 due to illness and died in 1939. The name of the court was changed eight times and is presently known as South Kern Municipal Court. John Steinbeck visited the Weedpatch Store, pictured here in the 1940s, while doing research for and filming of *The Grapes of Wrath*. (Courtesy of the Dust Bowl Foundation.)

One of the first farmers in the Vineland area was Peter Cattani. He and his family (pictured above) moved to the area in 1911. Peter was originally from Italy and married Henrietta Guerra in 1896. Their children were James, Kathryn, William ("Bill"), Arnold, and Madeline Cattani. Pictured below are Arnold Cattani Sr. (second from right) and his father, Peter Cattani (far right), in front of their home in Vineland. The Cattani family still occupies the home. (Both, courtesy of Sylvia and Arnold Cattani.)

Cotton was introduced to the Weedpatch area in 1917, contributing to the rise of California as the country's major cotton producer. By 1929, California cotton ranches, according to historian Devra Weber, outsized all others in the nation in terms of acreage, production, and number of workers. By that point, farms in Weedpatch had already been in production for over a decade. Calvin Alexander's son John G. Alexander and Wiley Giffen were the first cotton farmers in 1917. Pictured is a Mr. Phillips in a Weedpatch cotton field in 1924. (Courtesy of the Kern County Museum.)

Lloyd Frick arrived in California in 1919. He engaged in general and dairy farming in the Weedpatch area. He held leadership positions at the Agricultural Labor Bureau of San Joaquin Valley from 1928 to 1935, the California Pure Cotton Planting Seed Association, and the California Cotton Growers Association. Frick's General Farming office was located at 325 Third Avenue in the 1950s in Arvin. Pictured are Frick and two of his children, including Mary Lou (Frick) Thompson, the mother of Sylvia (Thompson) Cattani. Sylvia and her husband, Arnold Cattani, operate ranching, farming, real estate, and oil businesses in the area. (Courtesy of Sylvia and Arnold Cattani.)

The area boasts a rich agricultural history. People have farmed the fertile land here for over 130 years. In 1919, Joseph Di Giorgio purchased the Earl Fruit Company and 19,000 acres of land north of Arvin. The land was used to plant various crops, including alfalfa, plums, apricot, and peaches. Di Giorgio Farms grew into the Di Giorgio Fruit Corporation and became a major grower, packer, and shipper that employed thousands of people in the area. The women in this photograph are packing table grapes into wooden crates at a Di Giorgio packing shed in 1924. (Courtesy of the Arvin Historical Society.)

Pictured above on Peter Cattani's dairy farm, from right to left, are William "Bill" Cattani, Madeline Cattani, Richard Hosking, and Arnold Cattani. Bill and Arnold established the Cattani Brothers Cotton Gin in 1928 and the Cattani Brothers Farm in 1931. The Cattani Cotton Gin, pictured below in 1957, was one of the first six built in the area in 1937 on the corner of Sunset Avenue and Malaga Road. (Courtesy of Sylvia and Arnold Cattani.)

Agriculture has been the dominant industry in the Lamont area for decades. Migrant laborers from various parts of the world have toiled on the fertile land. Seen here are two men picking grapes in the Lamont area in 1936 and packing them into a wooden box that reads, "W.M. Buerkle," and "John J. Kovacevich Arvin, California." (Photograph by Dorothea Lange, courtesy of the Library of Congress.)

The large-scale operations at Di Giorgio farms required a massive pool of seasonal workers, both in the fields and the packing sheds. Here, a crew pusher poses with an all-female crew at the Di Giorgio packing shed in 1937. (Courtesy of Don Burkett.)

Di Giorgio farms was among the many local agricultural companies to face perennial strikes by its employees. In 1946, workers went on strike at Di Giorgio Farms to seek a living wage. Bertha McKee and Dovie Newsome are pictured picketing while enjoying lunch. The strike failed, and according to local historian Don Burkett, the workers were fired and business went on as usual. Di Giorgio farms became unionized in the 1960s, and its holdings were sold. (Courtesy of Don Burkett.)

Women constituted a major part of the agricultural workforce in the area, especially during the labor vacuum created by World War II. A Di Giorgio Farms crew made up of women is pictured here in 1946. The crew pusher (back row, third from right) is believed to be John Bohannon Harp, the grandfather of country music legend Merle Haggard. John and his wife Martha were longtime Lamont residents. (Courtesy of Don Burkett.)

There was a shortage of rubber during World War II. Guayule or synthetic rubber plants were grown in the area and somewhat alleviated the shortage. Guayule was grown near the Ribier Market on Di Giorgio Road between Arvin and Lamont. Pictured are wartime laborers working in guayule fields around 1944. (Courtesy of Don Burkett.)

In 1962, Cesar Chavez and Dolores Huerta formed the National Farm Workers Association (NFWA). They later organized alongside Filipino workers led by Philip Vera Cruz, Larry Itliong, and others. They rallied in support of better wages and working conditions. Ultimately, farm laborers organized across the country and carried out strikes. In 1966, the NFWA merged with the Agricultural Workers Organizing Committee to form the United Farm Workers (UFW). Pictured are union members participating in a grape strike in Lamont in 1973. (Courtesy of the Kern County Museum.)

Six

Migrations and Labor Camps

The Di Giorgio Post Office was located at the corner of Comanche Drive and Di Giorgio Road. At one point, there were 160 mailboxes available for use. Pictured is the Di Giorgio Post Office covered in snow around 1931. The sight is unique because snow is uncommon on the valley floor. (Courtesy of Don Burkett.)

Di Giorgio Farms was a mainstay of the local economy and operated multiple labor camps throughout the area. Pictured above are members of the Neal and McCoy families at the camp in 1937 posing in front of a grove and tent. Below, this view of what appears to be a boxcar camp around the 1930s includes rows of homes, power lines, and trees. (Above, courtesy of Labetta Glenn; below, courtesy of Don Burkett.)

By the 1920s, Mexicans were the primary source of labor for California's agriculture industry. Agricultural labor shortages in the United States during World War I led to the creation of guest worker programs. Historian Lori A. Flores noted that the first program was in place from 1917 to about 1922. An estimated 73,000 Mexican men worked in various industries, and some were subjected to abuse and violations of their contracts. According to historian Walter J. Stein, at least 150,000 Mexicans were working on farms in California in the 1920s. In the 1930s, "Okies" largely displaced Mexican workers. Pictured is a Mexican laborer plowing a field near Arvin. (Photograph by Dorothea Lange, courtesy of the Library of Congress.)

World War II created a renewed need for cheap labor, and the United States again looked to Mexico. The Bracero Program was in effect from 1942 to 1964. It is believed that more than five million Mexicans worked as *braceros*. In 1947, there were 130 braceros on Di Giorgio's payroll. Pictured are Mexican laborers at Di Giorgio Camp in the 1950s. Although the United States sought laborers, it simultaneously repatriated and deported over four million Mexican immigrants until the late 1950s. On local farms, crews of undocumented workers were hauled away and deported. (Courtesy of Carmen Marquez.)

Hundreds of workers lived at Di Giorgio camp year-round. Some of the youngest residents posed for this photograph at the camp in the 1940s. The school-aged children likely attended Rockpile School, which became Di Giorgio School in 1946. According to historian Ernesto Galarza, Di Giorgio set up separate camps and mess halls. The four halls housed white, Filipino, Mexican, and Japanese workers. During the season, hundreds of Mexican workers ate at a kitchen run by Carmen (Najera) and Lorenzo Marquez. (Courtesy of Don Burkett.)

Rubber was in demand during World War II, and the US government sought to meet the demand by setting up experimental guayule plantations. One was located near Ribier Market at Di Giorgio Road and Edison Drive (pictured). It may have been a branch of Camp Cooke. In 1944, the camp housed over 900 German and Japanese prisoners of war. The barracks are visible at top left. Prisoners picked cotton, sugar beets, and other crops for local farmers under contract with the US government. After the war, it was used as a farm labor camp. (Courtesy of Don Burkett.)

In the 1930s, extreme weather conditions and the Great Depression drove tens of thousands of people from the southern plains states of Oklahoma, Texas, Arkansas, and Missouri into California. The excitement about employment prospects quickly abated when migrants faced the reality that was illustrated in John Steinbeck's *The Grapes of Wrath*. For many families, shelter, food, and employment were unpredictable and often minimal. By the mid-1930s, the Resettlement Administration established labor camps to provide temporary shelter for migrants. The construction of the Arvin Federal Migratory Labor Camp (pictured above) and school began and was completed by 1936. The camp was constructed on 40 acres of land leased from Kern County purchased from Bertha Rankin. Initially, families lived in tents. By 1937, the Farm Security Administration was in charge of operating the camp. (Both photographs by Dorothea Lange, courtesy of the Library of Congress.)

The Arvin Federal Migratory Labor Camp has been known by many unofficial names. The name changes depending on the source. A few of the most common are Government Camp, Arvin Farm Labor Supply Center, and Weedpatch Camp. Presently, it is most frequently referred to as Sunset Camp. (Photograph by Dorothea Lange, courtesy of Library of Congress.)

The camp was run by government employees and self-governing councils that enforced rules the residents agreed to abide by. One well-liked camp manager was Tom Collins. He is pictured speaking with families at the camp in 1936. Collins was the camp manager to whom John Steinbeck dedicated *The Grapes of Wrath*. Dewey Russell and Fred Ross also worked as managers of the camp. Ross later became an influential labor organizer. (Both photographs by Dorothea Lange, courtesy of Library of Congress.)

Some residents were active in the administration of the camp. Dorothea Lange captured a Mother's Club meeting held at the camp in 1938. The topic of discussion was the bulk purchase of kerosene oil for the benefit of the community. Club members opened the meeting with a prayer and sang hymns. (Both photographs by Dorothea Lange, courtesy of Library of Congress.)

Over time, the Arvin Federal Migratory Camp grew to include tin cabins (pictured above), two-story apartments, and wooden and adobe houses. Below, children stand in front of the two-story apartments at the camp. A rental fee was imposed, but families that could not pay the fee were allowed to perform jobs around the camp to cover it. The revenue helped pay for camp supplies and activities. (Above, courtesy of the Dust Bowl Foundation; below, courtesy of Don Burkett.)

The camp had an office, post office, library, community center/recreational hall, laundry sinks, indoor sanitary units with running hot water, and a nursery. At left, young migrant children are cared for at the camp nursery/first-aid center while their parents labored in the fields. Dr. Delbert H. De Smet held clinics at the camp. Below, a young reader enjoys the library located at the camp. (Both photographs by Dorothea Lange, courtesy of Library of Congress.)

Over time, the Government Camp's recreational calendar included dances and other social activities. Children could enjoy playing in the recreational area (pictured). The camp was not idyllic, especially during the hot summer months, but it offered temporary relief for some. Those who grew up in labor camps as children often have different impressions and recollections of what camp life was like compared to their careworn parents who labored in the fields. Some of the children of Dust Bowl migrants still live in the area, but many have moved back "home" or to other parts of the United States. (Both photographs by Dorothea Lange, courtesy of the Library of Congress.)

In 1939, the Arvin co-op store and gas station was established near the entrance of the Arvin Federal Migratory Labor Camp. The shared plight of many of the camp residents also gave them a common resolve to improve their conditions together. It is believed that 60 residents of the camp established the co-op by contributing $1 each. (Both photographs by Dorothea Lange, courtesy of the National Archives.)

The migrant population that moved to the area persevered despite challenges such as unemployment, hunger, homelessness, and discrimination. Since 1936, thousands made the Government Camp their temporary home. Pictured above are Jimmy Phillips, Sue Risner holding Sharon Risner, unidentified, and Douglas Goforth being held by unidentified posing between tin cabins in 1948. At right (from left to right), W.C. Stampes, his mother, and brother Bobby are pictured inside their wooden cabin. They were originally from Oklahoma and arrived in California in 1944. (Above, courtesy of the Dust Bowl Foundation; right, courtesy of W.C. Stampes.)

When Dorothea Lange set about to capture images of Depression-era America, few could escape her lens. This included the two children seen here at a farm labor camp between Weedpatch and Lamont. Lange was one of a handful of photographers hired by the US government to document American life in the 1930s and 1940s as the nation transitioned from the Great Depression to World War II. She caught the nation's attention as she shed light on the lamentable living conditions of Dust Bowl migrants, especially as seen in the photograph of Florence Thompson, an image more popularly known as "Migrant Mother." Lange's extensive photograph collection includes images of life in Kern County. (Photograph by Dorothea Lange, courtesy of the National Archive.)

Bibliography

Boyd, William H. *Lower Kern River Country 1850–1950: Wilderness to Empire*. Bakersfield, CA: Kern County Historical Society, 1997.

Boyd, William Harland, John Ludeke, and Marjorie Rump (Ed). *Inside Historic Kern: Selections from the Kern County Historical Society's Quarterly, 1949–1981*. Bakersfield, CA: Kern County Historical Society, 1982.

Brewer, Chris. *Historic Kern County: An Illustrated History of Bakersfield and Kern County*. San Antonio, TX: Historical Publishing Network, 2001.

Burmeister, Eugene. *Below Bear Mountain: A Brief History of Arvin, DiGiorgio, Lamont and Weed Patch, Kern County, California*. Arvin, CA: Arvin Tiller-Booster, 1972.

————. *The Golden Empire: Kern County, California*. Beverly Hills, CA: Autograph Press, 1977.

Finch, Lynda W. and Rachel A. Arias. *150th Anniversary Kern County, Mexican Settlement 1866–2016 Volume II—The Legacy*. 2016.

Flores, Lori A. *Mexican Americans, Mexican Immigrants, and the California Farmworker Movement*. New Haven, CT: Yale University Press, 2016.

Galarza, Ernesto. *Spiders in the House and Workers in the Field*. South Bend, IN: University of Notre Dame Press, 1970.

Gavin, Camille. *Kern County Library, A Century of Progress*. Bakersfield, CA: Kern County Library, 2013.

Goldschmidt, Walter. *As You Sow*. New York, NY: Harcourt, Brace, and Co., 1947.

Gonzalez Jr., Juan L. *Mexican and Mexican American Farm Workers: The California Agricultural Industry*. New York, NY: Praeger, 1985.

Gregory, James. *American Exodus: The Dust Bowl Migration and Okie Culture in California*. New York, NY: Oxford University Press, 1991.

Kirkland, Jerry. *School District Origins in Kern County California*. Bakersfield, CA: Jerry Kirkland, 2010.

Stanley, Jerry. *Children of the Dust Bowl: The True Story of the School at Weedpatch Camp*. New York, NY: Crown, 1992.

Stein, Walter J. *California and the Dust Bowl Migration*. Westport, CT: Greenwood Press, 1973.

Weber, Devra. *Dark Sweat, White Gold: California Farm Workers, Cotton, and the New Deal*. Berkeley and Los Angeles, CA: University of California Press, 1996.

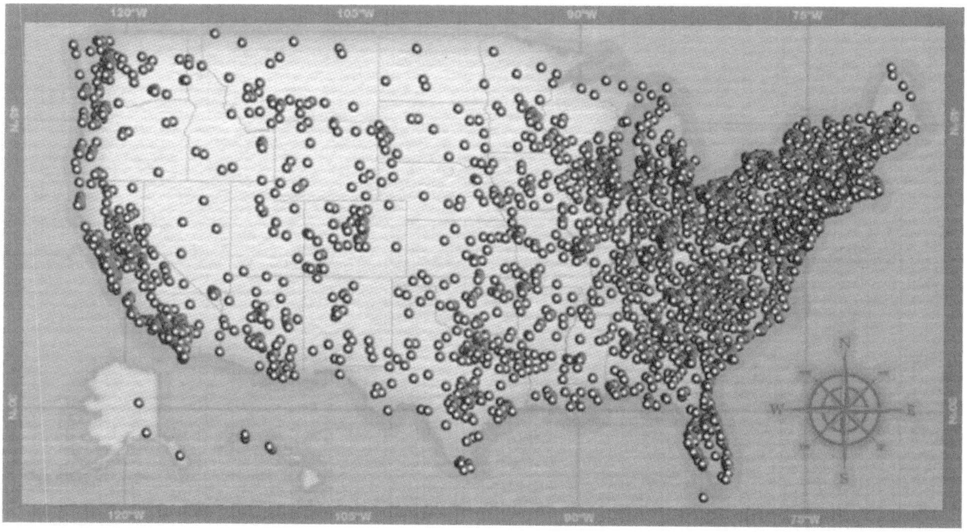

Consistent with our mission to preserve history on a local level, this book was printed in South Carolina on American-made paper and manufactured entirely in the United States. Products carrying the accredited Forest Stewardship Council (FSC) label are printed on 100 percent FSC-certified paper.